A Child of the 70's

Copyright © 2020 Adam Fisher

All rights reserved.

ISBN: 9781794244849
ISBN-13:

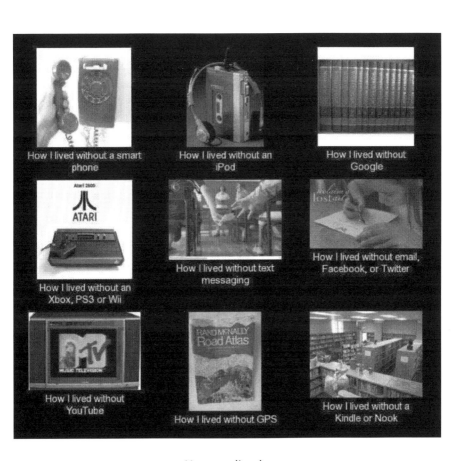

How we lived.

CONTENTS

1	The Tube	Pg 7
2	Country Earl's	Pg 25
3	Dark Side of the Alarm	Pg 54
4	Golden Skate	Pg 62
5	Pong	Pg 74
6	The Freedom Train	Pg 103
7	The Kang	Pg 109
8	Skynyrd	Pg 121
9	Radar Gun	Pg 133
10	Mean Green	Pg 146

"So Amy in Pensacola, here's your long distance dedication…"

"Keep your feet on the ground and keep reaching for the stars."

-Casey Kasem

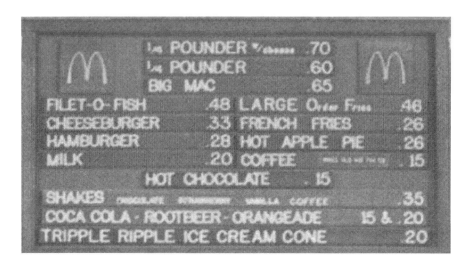

As seen in 1972.

Hear the numbers flip as the minutes pass by.

Chapter 1: The Tube

The 70's were a magical time. Technology, entertainment, and society at large was much simpler it seems. It was an internet-free world and we actually went outside to play. The first memory of watching TV was in July of 1969. This curious 3 year old got to see astronauts walk on the moon while he got a bowl haircut at a neighbor's house. He didn't realize the magnitude of what we were witnessing. Looking back, that was one of the most watched events in the history of television...right up there with O.J.'s Bronco chase.

One small step for man. One giant leap for TV viewership.

The TV set had an on/off button that also controlled the volume. When you turned the TV off, the screen would gradually grow dark and end up with a little white circle in the middle that would stay lit for a while until it eventually "died out".

The other two larger knobs on the front determined the channel. The top one could be turned to 13 numbers for VHF (regular) TV. Or you could turn that one to UHF and use the bottom knob to find stations on that bandwidth (known as "Ultra High Frequency").

UHF had PBS and the like, which was important because that's the one *"Sesame Street"* and *"The Electric Company"* were found on. Most of us had some aluminum foil affixed to the set's antenna to help with signal reception. Weather could definitely impact the signal quality, especially during important events...like when Evel Knievel tried to jump the Snake River Canyon. Thankfully, things got a lot better a decade later when cable was introduced into most neighborhoods.

When the broadcast day ended around 2 in the morning, John Wayne would voice over patriotic litany while an instrumental version of The National Anthem played. Then the station sign off concluded with technical difficulty vertical color bars on the screen and silence.

1970 COST OF LIVING

New House:	$23,450
Average Income:	$9,400
New Car:	$3,450
Minimum Wage:	$2.10/hour
Movie Ticket:	$1.55
Gasoline:	36 cents/gallon
Postage Stamp:	6 cents
Sugar:	39 cents/5 lbs
Milk:	62 cents/gallon
Coffee:	$1.90/pound
Eggs:	59 cents/dozen
Bread:	25 cents

At the movies

1970 by the numbers, in no particular order...

1. Patton

The World War II phase of the life of American General George S. Patton. *George C. Scott won The Academy Award for Best Actor.*

2. MASH

The staff of a Korean War field hospital use humor and hijinks to keep their sanity in the face of the horrors of war. *The movie was later turned into a successful TV series by the same name.*

3. The Aristocats

A clever tomcat leads the pack in an animated musical adventure set in turn of the century Paris. T*he movie's success was a great accomplishment for Walt Disney Productions.*

4. Kelly's Heroes

A group of U.S. Soldiers sneak across enemy lines to get their hands on a secret stash of Nazi treasure. *The Soundtrack included the Mike Curb song "All for the Love of Sunshine", which became the first #1 Country Music hit for Hank Williams, Jr.*

5. Little Big Man

Jack Crabb, looking back in extreme old age, tells of his life being raised by Native Americans and fighting with General Custer. *Chief Dan George earned an Academy Award Nomination for Best Supporting Actor.*

6. Tora! Tora! Tora!

In 1941, following an economic embargo of raw materials, Japan starts its war against the United States with a surprise attack on the American Naval Base, Pearl Harbor. *The film won the Academy Award for Best Special Effects.*

7. Five Easy Pieces

A dropout from upper-class America picks up work along the way on oil rigs when his life isn't spent in a squalid succession of bars, motels, and other points of interest. *Jack Nicholson earned an Academy Award Nomination for Best Actor.*

8. Catch-22

A man is trying desperately to be certified insane during World War II, so he can stop flying missions. *The film had a real casualty* as Second Unit Director John Jordan refused to wear a harness during a bomber scene and fell out of the open tail turret 4,000 ft. to his death.

9. El Topo

A mysterious black-clad gunfighter wanders around a mystical Western Landscape encountering multiple bizarre characters. *The film employed maimed and dwarf performers to enhance its strange theme.*

10. Two Mules for Sister Sara

Nun Sara is on the run in Mexico and is saved from cowboys by Hogan, who is preparing for a future mission to capture a French Fort. The pair become good friends, but Sara never does tell him the true reason behind her being outlawed. *Many of the cast and crew were stricken by illness while filming due to the adjustment to the food and water in Mexico.*

Honorable Mentions:

Love Story

Harvard elitist Oliver meets working class Jenny and they fall in love despite their differences. *The film had 7 Academy Award Nominations including Best Picture, but its sole winner was for Best Musical Score. It also popularized the catchphrase, "Love means never having to say you're sorry".*

Woodstock

A documentary of the counter culture music festival held on Max Yasgur's Farm in rural upstate New York in 1969. *Not surprisingly, and with the aid of Jimi Hendrix playing "The Star-Spangled Banner", it won the Academy Award for Best Documentary.*

Airport

A bomber on board a commercial airliner is the plot line for this first of many "epic" disaster movies the 1970's had to offer. *The film garnered ten Academy Award Nominations, including Best PIcture, with Helen Hayes winning the Oscar for Best Supporting Actress.*

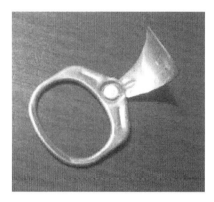

In the 70's, can tops were pull-off. Beware bare feet.

For the ears

1970 Rock by the numbers, in no particular order...

On the Turntable
1. **John Lennon/Plastic Ono Band** - John Lennon
2. **Morrison Hotel** - The Doors
3. **Bridge Over Troubled Water** - Simon & Garfunkel
4. **Déjà Vu** - Crosby, Stills, Nash, and Young
5. **American Beauty** – The Grateful Dead
6. **Let It Be** - The Beatles
7. **Layla And Other Assorted Love Songs** - Derek and The Dominos
8. **Live At Leeds** - The Who
9. **After The Gold Rush** - Neil Young

10. **Paranoid** - Black Sabbath
11. **Led Zeppelin III** - Led Zeppelin
12. **Moondance** - Van Morrison
13. **Cosmo's Factory** - Creedence Clearwater Revival
14. **Workingman's Dead** – The Grateful Dead
15. **Sweet Baby James** - James Taylor

On the Radio
1. **Layla** - Derek and the Dominos
2. **Bridge Over Troubled Water** - Simon and Garfunkel
3. **Let It Be** - The Beatles
4. **Your Song** - Elton John
5. **Get Up (I Feel Like Being A) Sex Machine** - James Brown
6. **Lola** - The Kinks
7. **Who'll Stop the Rain** - Creedence Clearwater Revival
8. **Fire and Rain** - James Taylor
9. **Paranoid** - Black Sabbath
10. **All Right Now** - Free

On the tube 1970

1. All My Children (1970–2011)

Set in the fictional East Coast suburb Pine Valley, All My Children is the decades-old, risk-taking soap that centers around Erica Kane and her long line of husbands.

2. UFO (1970–1973)

The missions of the Supreme Headquarters Alien Defence Organization, which defends Earth from extra-terrestrial threats.

3. Mary Tyler Moore (1970–1977)

The lives and trials of a young single woman and her friends, both at work and at home.

4. The Partridge Family (1970–1974)

The humorous adventures of a family of pop musicians.

5. Tatort (1970–)

A long running German cop show, where detectives work to solve a crime.

6. The Odd Couple (1970–1975)

Two men, a neat freak and a slob separated from their wives, have to live together despite their differences.

7. McCloud (1970–1977)

Sam McCloud is a Marshal from Taos, New Mexico, who takes a temporary assignment in the New York City Police Department. His keen sense of detail and detecting subtle clues, learned from his experience, enable him to nab unsuspecting criminals despite his unbelieving boss.

8. A Family at War (1970–1972)

The lower middle class Ashton family of the city of Liverpool deal with life on the home front during the Second World War.

9. The Goodies (1970–1982)

The Goodies are a three man agency whose brief is to do 'anything, anytime'. This gave the series carte blanche to do whatsoever it pleased, with a cartoon-like surrealism.

10. Nanny and the Professor (1970–1971)

Ever-cheerful Nanny helps the Everett family with her subtly magical abilities, such as seemingly reading minds, seeing the future or making fortunate coincidences happen.

Honorable Mention:

21. NFL Monday Night Football (1970–)

Coverage of professional football featuring teams from the National Football League airing on Monday nights during the NFL's regular season.

> **What in the world 1970**
>
> U.S. President Richard Nixon orders an invasion of Cambodia, widening the war in Vietnam. In protest, millions march across the U.S., and university campuses are shut down by student strikes. Four protestors at Kent State University in Ohio are killed by National Guard troops.

Bubble gum contained comics.

*Bell bottom blues, you made me cry.
I don't want to lose this feeling.
And if I could choose a place to die.
It would be in your arms.*
　　-Eric Clapton, 1971

The most popular book of 1971.

Apollo 15's Lunar Rover. Cruise till the tires fall off.

We heard *"American Pie"* for the first time in 1972...lamenting Buddy Holly's untimely death in a plane crash that seemingly ended the golden age of rock and roll. But it survived and thrived.

Sunday night after suffering through "Lawrence Welk".

Top TV Shows of 1970   (as measured by Nielsen Media Research)

1	*Marcus Welby, M.D.*	ABC
2	*The Flip Wilson Show*	NBC
3	*Here's Lucy*	CBS
4	*Ironside*	NBC
5	*Gunsmoke*	CBS
6	*ABC Movie of the Week*	ABC
7	*Hawaii Five-O*	CBS
8	*Medical Center*	
9	*Bonanza*	NBC
10	*The F.B.I.*	ABC
11	*The Mod Squad*	
12	*Adam-12*	
13	*Rowan & Martin's Laugh-In*	NBC
	The Wonderful World of Disney	
15	*Mayberry R.F.D.*	
16	*Hee Haw*	CBS
17	*Mannix*	
18	*The Men from Shiloh*	NBC
19	*My Three Sons*	CBS
20	*The Doris Day Show*	
21	*The Smith Family*	ABC
22	*The Mary Tyler Moore Show*	CBS
23	*NBC Saturday Movie*	NBC
24	*The Dean Martin Show*	

The "Astro Twin" in Greenville, South Carolina.

"Modern" manual typewriter.

What in the world 1970

The Beatles break up. All four musicians - John, Paul, George, & Ringo - go on to successful solo careers.

At the movies

1971 by the numbers, in no particular order...

1. Willy Wonka & The Chocolate Factory

A poor but hopeful boy seeks one of the five coveted golden tickets that will send him on a tour of Willy Wonka's Mysterious Chocolate Factory. *The film introduced the song "The Candy Man", which become a popular hit for Sammy Davis Jr.*

2. A Clockwork Orange

In a dystopian future Britain Society, a sadistic gang leader, Alex, is imprisoned and volunteers for a conduct-aversion experiment, but it doesn't go as planned. *The dark humor film earned Stanley Kubrick Academy Award Nominations for Best Picture, Best Director, and Best Adapted Screenplay.*

3. The Last Picture Show

In 1951, a group of high schoolers come of age in a bleak, isolated, atrophied West Texas town that is slowly dying, both culturally and economically. *The black and white film earned the Academy Award for Best Supporting Actor (Ben Johnson) and Best Supporting Actress (Cloris Leachman), and was also Nominated for Best Picture.*

4. Dirty Harry

A San Francisco Police Inspector is assigned to track down a serial killer named Scorpio. *The film introduced America to hard-nosed cop "Dirty Harry" Callahan (Clint Eastwood), and would go on to make four successful sequels.*

5. Bedknobs and Broomsticks

An apprentice witch, three kids, and a cynical magician cast spells and ride brooms. *It won the Academy Award for Best Special Visual Effects.*

6. Fiddler on the Roof

In Prerevolutionary Russia, a Jewish peasant contends with marrying off three of his daughters while there is growing anti-Semitic sentiment threatening his village. *The film won three Academy Awards, including Best Music, Scoring Adaptation and*

Original Song Score for arranger-conductor John Williams, and was nominated for several others including Best Picture, Best Actor, and Best Supporting Actor.

7. Billy Jack

An Indian foot-fighter and Green Beret Vietnam War Veteran defends the Freedom School from a corrupt gang of townsfolk. *Tom Laughlin starred in, directed. and co-wrote the script.*

8. Carnal Knowledge

The story follows the sexual exploits of two college roommates over a 25-year period, from the late 1940s to the early 1970s. *The film starred Art Garfunkel and Jack Nicholson, and won Ann-Margret the Academy Award for Best Supporting Actress.*

9. The French Connection

A pair of NYC Cops in the Narcotics Bureau stumble onto a drug smuggling job with a French Connection. *The film won four Academy Awards including Best Film and Best Actor for Gene Hackman, who played "Popeye" Doyle.*

10. Diamonds Are Forever

A diamond smuggling investigation leads James Bond to Las Vegas, where he uncovers an evil plot involving a rich business tycoon. *This was Sean Connery's last appearance as Bond, who was replaced by Roger Moore as the movie series continued.*

Honorable Mention:

The Omega Man

Charlton Heston is the presumed lone survivor of a global

pandemic who uses his wits - and machine guns - to protect his way of life from murderous Zombies. *The film remains popular as a science fiction cult classic.*

For the ears

1971 Rock by the numbers, in no particular order...

On the Turntable
1. **Sticky Fingers** - The Rolling Stones
2. **Led Zeppelin IV** - Led Zeppelin
3. **L.A. Woman** - The Doors
4. **Aqualung** - Jethro Tull
5. **Who's Next** - The Who
6. **At Fillmore East** - The Allman Brothers Band
7. **Imagine** - John Lennon
8. **Tapestry** - Carole King
9. **Every Picture Tells A Story** - Rod Stewart
10. **Meddle** - Pink Floyd
11. **What's Going On** - Marvin Gaye
12. **The Concert For Bangla Desh** - Various Artists
13. **Tupelo Honey** - Van Morrison
14. **4 Way Street** - Crosby, Stills, Nash & Young
15. **Madman Across The Water** - Elton John

On the Radio
1. **Stairway to Heaven** - Led Zeppelin
2. **Imagine** - John Lennon
3. **What's Going On** - Marvin Gaye
4. **Let's Stay Together** - Al Green
5. **Maggie May** - Rod Stewart

6. **American Pie** - Don McLean
7. **Won't Get Fooled Again** - The Who
8. **Brown Sugar** - The Rolling Stones
9. **Just My Imagination** - The Temptations
10. **Family Affair** - Sly and the Family Stone

> **What in the world 1971**
>
> The microprocessor – the foundation of today's computers – is introduced.

Advertised as "the real thing". Coca-Cola in glass bottles.

Chapter 2: Country Earl's

"Fish Is Brain Food. Bring A Dumb Friend And Eat Often."

That was the verbiage on the big sign in the lobby at Country Earl's "Stompin and Chompin" Restaurant. It was an old fashioned fish camp, proudly residing "in the middle of nowhere," as its owner proclaimed. Really it was located in Simpsonville S.C., behind Bethel Elementary School and bordering a rural neighborhood that many of my classmates and friends lived in.

We loved that place. The moment you sat down, they would bring a basket of hot hushpuppies to the table. They had the best fried chicken in the world. Located throughout the dining hall were Old-West type signs that told about historical criminal figures like the Dalton Gang, Jesse James, and Belle Starr. Learning history was fun at Country Earl's.

The owner also dabbled in the music business. Country Earl Baughman was a local radio personality/disc jockey for many years, with numerous upstate radio stations including WESC, WCKI, WFIS, WBBR, WAGI and WOLT where he hosted his *"Country Earl's Country Classics Radio Show."* He started his career in the 1950's and continued until the 2000's.

We would sometimes listen to his show on WESC (am 660 kHz), whose tag line was *"Six Sixty in Dixie"*. Country Earl was also an accomplished musician and songwriter and was inducted into the Rockabilly Hall Of Fame. I remember they had "45" records for sale at the restaurant. He passed away in 2012 at seventy-nine years old, but fond memories of him will live forever.

A Country Earl "45" single.

What in the world 1971

Apollo 15 lands on the moon and uses the Lunar Rover for the first time.

On the tube 1971

1. Columbo (1971–2003)

Los Angeles homicide detective Lieutenant Columbo uses his humble ways and bumbling demeanor to solve even the most well-concealed of crimes.

2. The Waltons (1971–1981)

The life and trials of a 1930s and 1940s Virginia mountain family through financial depression and World War II.

3. All in the Family (1971–1979)

A working class man constantly squabbles with his family over the important issues of the day.

4. Alias Smith and Jones (1971–1973)

Hannibal Heyes and Kid Curry, two of the most wanted outlaws in the history of the West, are popular "with everyone except the railroads and the banks".

5. Upstairs, Downstairs (1971–1975)

The trials of the British aristocratic Bellamy family and their household staff.

6. Cannon (1971–1976)

Frank Cannon is an overweight, balding ex-cop with a deep voice and expensive tastes in culinary pleasures; he becomes a high-priced private investigator.

7. The Persuaders! (1971–1972)

Two worlds collide when the titled Englishman, Lord Brett Sinclair, and the Bronx-raised, self-made American Danny Wilde, reluctantly join forces to right wrongs, and to protect the innocent.

8. McMillan & Wife (1971–1977)

San Francisco Police Commissioner Stewart "Mac" McMillan and his amateur detective wife keep their marriage unpredictable while solving the city's most baffling crimes.

9. Great Performances (1971–)

"You Can't Take It With You" is hailed one of the greatest revivals and filmed plays for PBS television. David Woods brought stunning charm, humor, and time to this Moss Hart masterpiece.

10. The Electric Company (1971–1977)

A comedy variety show that teaches basic phonetic and grammar concepts using live-action sketches, cartoons, and songs. It helped launch the career of celebrities like Morgan Freeman.

Honorable Mentions:

Soul Train (1971–)

A pop music dance show with an African-American focus.

The Sonny and Cher Comedy Hour (1971–1974)

After a string of successful hit records, Sonny and Cher attempted to take the movie world by storm. After they failed in that attempt, they regrouped and refashioned, blossoming into a cabaret act that found success in nightclubs. Their easy banter and famous names led to them getting their own television variety show in the 1970's.

Credit Card cutting edge technology.

America's favorite junkmen.

Mikey likes it. Life Cereal 1971.

We were throwing the football in the front yard as the teenagers in the neighborhood talked about how awesome the new Led Zeppelin album was (the fourth album, *"IV"*).

<u>Saturday Morning Cartoons Fan Favorites</u>
Road Runner vs Wile E. Coyote
Hong Kong Phooey
Fat Albert
Scooby-Doo
Bugs Bunny
The Jetsons

Top TV Shows of 1971   (as measured by Nielsen Media Research)

1	*All in the Family*	CBS
2	*The Flip Wilson Show*	NBC
3	*Marcus Welby, M.D.*	ABC
4	*Gunsmoke*	CBS
5	ABC Movie of the Week	ABC
6	*Sanford and Son*	NBC
7	*Mannix*	CBS
8	*Funny Face*	CBS
8	*Adam-12*	NBC
10	*The Mary Tyler Moore Show*	CBS
11	*Here's Lucy*	CBS
12	*Hawaii Five-O*	CBS
13	*Medical Center*	CBS
14	*The NBC Mystery Movie*	NBC
15	*Ironside*	NBC
16	*The Partridge Family*	ABC
17	*The F.B.I.*	ABC
18	*The New Dick Van Dyke Show*	CBS
19	*The Wonderful World of Disney*	NBC
20	*Bonanza*	NBC
21	*The Mod Squad*	ABC
22	*Rowan & Martin's Laugh-In*	NBC
23	*The Carol Burnett Show*	CBS
23	*The Doris Day Show*	CBS
25	*Monday Night Football*	ABC

Littering was no laughing matter in this TV ad.

Blacklight Posters lit up the walls.

Label sold product.

*Newsman Walter Cronkite was talking about the Gulf of Tonkin.
Yet we were waiting on the commercial for Tonka Trucks.*

*"They're all gone..." broadcaster Jim McKay said
to a worldwide audience.*

Eleven Israeli athletes are killed at the
Munich Olympic Games in 1972.
Five terrorists and one policeman are also killed.
The world's war on terror was just getting started.

At the movies

1972 by the numbers, in no particular order…

1. The Godfather

The aging patriarch of an organized crime dynasty transfers control of his clandestine empire to his reluctant son. *The film earned nine Academy Award Nominations and won three, including Best Picture, Best Actor (Marlon Brando), and Best Adapted Screenplay for Mario Puzo and Francis Ford Coppola. Many feel that this, and the following sequel, are the two best movies ever made.*

2. Deliverance

Intent on seeing the Cahulawassee River before it's dammed and turned into a lake, outdoor fanatic Lewis Medlock takes his friends canoeing into the dangerous American back-country…a trip they'll never forget. *The iconic "Dueling Banjos" scene helped earn the film three Academy Award Nominations, including Best Picture.*

3. Young Winston

Complex family relationships, as well as a combat experience, form the personality of the future world-famous politician and leader of Great Britain. *The film had Nominations for three Academy Awards, including Best Set Decoration and Best Costume Design.*

4. Last Tango in Paris

A young Parisian woman meets a middle-aged American Businessman who demands their clandestine relationship be based only on sex. *It earned an Academy Award Nomination for Marlon Brando as Best Actor.*

5. The Way of the Dragon

A man visits his relatives at their restaurant in Italy and has to help them defend against brutal gangsters harassing them. *The film helped launch the careers of martial arts legends Bruce Lee and Chuck Norris.*

6. Cabaret

A female girlie club entertainer in pre WWII Berlin romances two men while the Nazi Party rises to power around them. *This movie won eight Academy Awards, including Best Director for Bob Fosse and Best Actress for Liza Minnelli.*

7. The Last House on the Left

Two teenage girls head to a rock concert for one's birthday. While trying to score marijuana in the city, they are kidnapped and brutalized by a gang of psychotic convicts. *The film helped launch the career of Writer/Director Wes Craven, who would later create the "Nightmare on Elm Street" series of movies.*

8. Jeremiah Johnson

A mountain man who wishes to live the life of a hermit becomes the unwilling object of a long vendetta by Indians, and proves to be a match for their warriors in one-on-one combat on the early frontier. *Director Sydney Pollack said it took him over two weeks to photograph the sequence starring an actual 600-pound grizzly bear.*

9. The Poseidon Adventure

Nine people explore a cruise ship at sea in a manner that turns their whole lives upside down. *The film won five Academy Awards, including Best Music/Original Song for "The Morning After".*

10. Pink Flamingos

Notorious Baltimore criminal Divine goes up against a sleazy married couple who make an attempt to humiliate her and seize her tabloid-given title as "The Filthiest Person Alive". *This American exploitation, black comedy film, was directed, written, produced, narrated, filmed, and edited by John Waters, and is widely considered his best work.*

Honorable Mention:

What's Up, Doc?

Identical plaid overnight bags get mixed up in San Francisco and create a romantic screwball comedy. *One iconic scene has actress Barbra Streisand imitating Humphrey Bogart with the line, "Of all the gin joints, in all the towns, in all the world....he walks into mine. Play it again, Sam."*

Sister's 70's bike. Style not uncommon.

You just don't see these coin holders very much anymore.

> **What in the world 1972**
>
> The Rolling Stones rent a house in France and record their double album *"Exile on Main Street"* in the basement.

For the ears

1972 Rock by the numbers, in no particular order…

On the Turntable
1. **Exile On Main Street** - The Rolling Stones
2. **Talking Book** – Stevie Wonder
3. **Ziggy Stardust And The Spiders From Mars** – David Bowie
4. **Thick As A Brick** - Jethro Tull
5. **Eat a Peach** - The Allman Brothers Band
6. **Harvest** – Neil Young
7. **Machine Head** – Deep Purple
8. **The Harder They Come** – Jimmy Cliff
9. **Transformer** – Lou Reed
10. **Let's Stay Together** – Al Green
11. **What's Going On** - Marvin Gaye
12. **St. Dominic's Preview** – Van Morrison
13. **Superfly** – Curtis Mayfield
14. **Europe '72** – The Grateful Dead
15. **Honky Chateau** - Elton John

On the Radio

1. **Superstition** - Stevie Wonder
2. **Papa Was a Rollin' Stone** - The Temptations
3. **Smoke on the Water** - Deep Purple
4. **Lean on Me** - Bill Withers
5. **Heart of Gold** - Neil Young
6. **Walk on the Wild Side** - Lou Reed
7. **You Are the Sunshine of My Life** - Stevie Wonder
8. **If You Don't Know Me by Now** - Harold Melvin & Blue Notes
9. **I'll Take You There** - The Staple Singers
10. **Tumbling Dice** - The Rolling Stones

On the tube 1972

1. M*A*S*H (1972–1983)

The staff of an Army hospital in the Korean War find that laughter is the best way to deal with their situation.

2. Emmerdale (1972–)

A soap opera set in a fictional village in the Yorkshire Dales.

3. Sanford and Son (1972–1977)

The misadventures of a cantankerous junk dealer and his frustrated son living in the Watts neighborhood of Los Angeles.

4. Are You Being Served? (1972–1985)

The misadventures of the staff of a retail floor of a major department store.

5. Emergency! (1972–1979)

The crew of Los Angeles County Fire Department Station 51,

particularly the paramedic team, and Rampart Hospital respond to emergencies in their operating area.

6. Kung Fu (1972–1975)

The adventures of a Shaolin Monk as he wanders the American West armed only with his skill in Kung Fu.

7. The Streets of San Francisco (1972–1977)

A veteran cop with more than twenty years of experience is teamed with a young Inspector to solve crimes in San Francisco, California.

8. The Bob Newhart Show (1972–1978)

The professional and personal misadventures of a psychologist and his family, patients, friends and colleagues.

9. Maude (1972–1978)

This "All In The Family" spin-off centers around Edith's cousin, Maude Findlay. She's a liberal, independent woman living in Tuckahoe, NY with her fourth husband Walter.

10. The Price Is Right (1972–)

Contestants compete for prizes and cash, including cars and vacations, in games that test their knowledge of consumer goods pricing.

Honorable Mention:

The Midnight Special (1972–1981)

Late night rock and pop music performances are featured.

Hot Wheels. Configure for speed.

A real crowd pleaser.

*Mr. Doohickey.
A beloved character from the locally broadcast Children's show "Monty's Rascals".*

Defrost the freezer...or maybe just use a steak knife on it.

Top TV Shows of 1972   (as measured by Nielsen Media Research)

1	All in the Family	CBS
2	Sanford and Son	NBC
3	Hawaii Five-O	
4	Maude	CBS
5	Bridget Loves Bernie	
	The NBC Sunday Mystery Movie	NBC
7	The Mary Tyler Moore Show	CBS
	Gunsmoke	
9	The Wonderful World of Disney	
10	Ironside	
		NBC
11	Adam-12	
12	The Flip Wilson Show	
13	Marcus Welby, M.D.	ABC
14	Cannon	
15	Here's Lucy	CBS
16	The Bob Newhart Show	
17	Tuesday Movie of the Week	
18	Monday Night Football	ABC
	The Partridge Family	
19	The Waltons	
	Medical Center	CBS
22	The Carol Burnett Show	
23	ABC Sunday Movie	ABC
	The Rookies	
	Barnaby Jones	CBS
25	The Little People	NBC
	ABC Wednesday Movie of the Week	ABC

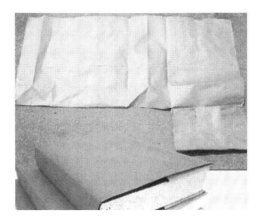

Grocery store paper bags were used as book covers.

> **What in the world 1972**
>
> Five men, going by the code name "The Plumbers", are caught breaking in to the Watergate Complex where the Democratic Party offices are – the start of the Watergate Scandal.

Welcome to the Machine

Second hand smoke was everywhere, and cigarette machines could be found in the lobby of most restaurants and hotels.

Across the Field

We walked to Bethel Elementary School. First leg of the journey took us through our front yard and down a big hill past the neighbor's yard which ended at a creek. There we found just enough rocks in a row to make a jumping trip across without getting wet.

Then it was about a hundred yards up a steep path through the woods. At the top of that trail there was a graveyard, which was very old based on the dates on some of the headstones...many prior to the Civil War. There was a church at the edge of the property, and once we crossed that yard there was Holland Road - a rural two lane special.

Next was a really large soybean field, probably a quarter mile or so. And after tromping through that was Bethel Elementary. The soybean field is now Highway I-385 and all the woods are neighborhoods and houses. Bethel has been modernized and continues to educate the young people.

At the movies

1973 by the numbers, in no particular order…

1. The Exorcist

When a teenage girl is possessed by a mysterious entity, her mother seeks the help of two priests to save her daughter. *The Horror Film earned ten Academy Award Nominations and garnered wins for Best Picture, Best Actress (Ellen Burstyn), Best Supporting Actor (Jason Miller), and Best Supporting Actress (Linda Blair).*

2. Papillon

Two criminals, serving their sentence on a dreadful prison island, plot an escape. *Steve McQueen and Dustin Hoffman were superb as the main characters in this film based on a true story.*

3. American Graffiti

A couple of high school grads spend one final night cruising the strip with their buddies before they go off to college. *The film was Nominated for five Academy Awards, including Best Director for George Lucas, who would later be responsible for "Star Wars".*

4. The Sting

In 1936, at the height of the Great Depression, two grifters team up to pull off the ultimate con. *This movie won six Academy Awards, including Best Picture, Best Director, and Best Actor (Robert Redford).*

5. The Holy Mountain

In a corrupt, greed-fueled world, a powerful alchemist leads a

Christ-like character and seven materialistic figures to the Holy Mountain, where they hope to achieve enlightenment. *The film's Writer, Director, and Main Character was Alexandro Jodorowsky.*

6. High Plains Drifter

A gunfighting stranger comes to the small town of Lago and is hired to bring the townsfolk together, in an attempt to hold off three outlaws who are on their way. *Clint Eastwood directed and starred in this action packed thriller.*

7. Enter the Dragon

A martial artist agrees to spy on a reclusive crime lord using his invitation to a tournament there as cover. *The film's star, Bruce Lee, died unexpectedly in Hong Kong three weeks before the movie premiered in 1973.*

8. Westworld

A robot malfunction creates havoc and terror for unsuspecting vacationers at a futuristic amusement park. *Yul Brynner is outstanding as "The Gunslinger" in Michael Crichton's directorial debut.*

9. Soylent Green

In the future world, ravaged by the greenhouse effect and overpopulation, an NYPD detective investigates the secret ingredient found in the primary food source. *This was the 101st, and also the last, movie in which the great Edward G. Robinson appeared… twelve days after the completion of filming he died of cancer.*

10. Serpico

An honest New York cop named Frank Serpico blows the whistle on rampant corruption in the force, only to have his comrades turn against him. *Al Pacino earned an Academy Award Nomination for Best Actor as he continued to rise as a premier actor in the decades to come.*

Honorable Mentions:

Walking Tall

Based on the life of Tennessee Sheriff Buford Pusser, who almost single handedly cleaned up his small town of crime and corruption…but it came at a personal cost of his family life and nearly his life. *This movie became a cult classic with two direct sequels of its own, a TV Movie, a brief TV Series, and a remake that had its own two sequels.*

The Way We Were

Two people are madly in love until their political views and personal convictions drive them apart. *The film garnered six Academy Award Nominations, winning Best Music/Original Song for the title track (Marvin Hamlisch).*

Paper Moon

During the Great Depression, a con man finds himself saddled with a young girl, and the two forge an unlikely partnership to turn a profit. *Tatum O'Neal won the Academy Award for Best Supporting Actress, an astounding feat considering she was only ten years old during filming.*

*ATM's are non existent...we stop at the bank for Mom to cash a check.
Go to McAlister Square Mall where the only Chick-Fil-A was located in our city.*

Pure Evel. The Stunt Cycle was the most iconic toy of the 70's.

A storefront seen in most malls in the 1970's.

Good old "Simpleville", South Carolina

> **What in the world 1973**
>
> The mobile phone is invented.

Paper Drive

The newspaper was delivered daily in haphazard fashion on our front lawn...in a plastic bag, formerly containing a loaf of bread, to shield it from the elements. We saved our newspapers after reading them. Rather, after my parents read them. We had no use for them or their content. That would change as we got older. But we would have stacks and stacks cluttering every corner of the garage. Once in a while, the school would have what was called a paper drive. We loaded up the station wagon with old newspapers and even some brown paper bags from the grocery store. Took them to Bethel Elementary School and did our part to recycle. Never mind that it took seven gallons of gas to get there.

Family vacation at Carowinds. The park opened March 31, 1973

Brain Child of Charlotte businessman Earl Patterson Hall, who was inspired to build the park by a 1956 trip to Disneyland and a dream of bringing the two states of N.C. and S.C. closer together.

"Thunder Road"

For the ears

1973 Rock by the numbers, in no particular order...

On the Turntable
1. **Dark Side Of The Moon** – Pink Floyd
2. **Houses Of The Holy** – Led Zeppelin
3. **Quadrophenia** – The Who
4. **Innervisions** – Stevie Wonder
5. **Band On The Run** – Paul McCartney and Wings
6. **Aladdinsane** – David Bowie
7. **(pronounced 'lĕh-'nérd 'skin-'nérd)** – Lynyrd Skynyrd
8. **The Harder They Come** – Jimmy Cliff
9. **Let's Get It On** – Marvin Gaye
10. **Catch A Fire** – Bob Marley and the Wailers
11. **Tres Hombres** – ZZ Top
12. **Goats Head Soup** – The Rolling Stones
13. **Aerosmith** – Aerosmith
14. **Mind Games** – John Lennon
15. **Goodbye Yellow Brick Road** - Elton John

On the Radio
1. **Free Bird** - Lynyrd Skynyrd
2. **Let's Get It On** - Marvin Gaye
3. **Midnight Train to Georgia** - Gladys Knight and the Pips
4. **Dream On** - Aerosmith
5. **Living for the City** - Stevie Wonder
6. **Money** - Pink Floyd
7. **Piano Man** - Billy Joel
8. **Killing Me Softly with His Song** - Roberta Flack
9. **Goodbye Yellow Brick Road** - Elton John
10. **That Lady** - Isley Brothers

Meaner than a junkyard dog...

What in the world 1973

The U.S. Supreme Court rules on Roe v. Wade, legalizing abortion.

Library Card Catalog...the original Google.

Chapter 3: Dark Side of the Alarm

My lawn mowing service money was spent at the local record store...Camelot Music at the mall. At the suggestion of many friends, Pink Floyd's *"Dark Side of the Moon"* album was one of my first purchases. It was beyond description then and it's beyond description now. When it was bed time, I would plug in the headphones to the stereo and put on that record. Just when you were about to zonk out, one track on the album would go crazy with a bunch of clock alarms going off. Such a startling effect would have me jump up wondering what was going on, and that jump would accidently pull the headphones plug out of the stereo – making the music blast throughout the house, much to the dismay of the other sleepers.

On the tube 1973

1. The Young and the Restless (1973–)

Set in Genoa City, this is the long-running soap that tells the story of the struggle behind the business, and sex-savvy Abbott and Newman clans.

2. Last of the Summer Wine (1973–2010)

Three old men from Yorkshire who have never grown up face the trials of their fellow town citizens and everyday life and stay young by reminiscing about the days of their youth and attempting feats not common to the elderly.

3. Match Game (1973–1982)

The five-day-a-week syndicated successor to the popular CBS game show, where two could compete to match fill-in-the-blank phrases with those of the celebrities.

4. The World at War (1973–1976)

A groundbreaking 26-part documentary series narrated by the actor Laurence Olivier about the deadliest conflict in history, World War II.

5. Kojak (1973–1978)

A bald, lollipop sucking police detective with a fiery righteous attitude battles crime in his city.

6. Thriller (1973–1976)

Anthology series of self-contained episodes with the genres ranging from murder mystery to suspense to psychological and supernatural horror.

7. Barnaby Jones (1973–1980)

The exploits of milk-swilling, geriatric private eye Barnaby Jones.

8. Some Mothers Do 'Ave 'Em (1973–1978)

Accident-prone Frank Spencer fails to navigate the simplest tasks of daily life, while also trying to look after his wife and baby.

9. Star Trek: The Animated Series (1973–1975)

The further adventures of Captain James T. Kirk and the crew of the USS Enterprise, as they explore the galaxy and defend the United Federation of Planets.

10. The Tomorrow People (1973–1979)

The Tomorrow People are British teens who have special powers. They can communicate to each other using telepathy. They can also transport themselves (they call it "Jaunting").

Honorable Mention:

Schoolhouse Rock! (1973–2009)

A series of shorts illustrating various songs that teach multiplication tables, grammar, science, American history, computers, economics, and environmentalism.

"Conjunction Junction what's your function?..."

Schoolhouse Rock tricked us into learning math and grammar and politics with catchy songs and animated heroes like "Bill", who would one day reach manhood and become a Law.

"Snail Mail" was the only game in town for written communication.

Best part of the Sunday newspaper – the comics.

Fifty cents use to actually buy something.

Top TV Shows of 1973   (as measured by Nielsen Media Research)

1	*All in the Family*	CBS
2	*The Waltons*	
3	*Sanford and Son*	NBC
4	*M*A*S*H*	
5	*Hawaii Five-O*	
6	*Maude*	
7	*Kojak*	CBS
	The Sonny & Cher Comedy Hour	
9	*The Mary Tyler Moore Show*	
	Cannon	
11	*The Six Million Dollar Man*	ABC
12	*The Bob Newhart Show*	CBS
	The Wonderful World of Disney	NBC
14	*The NBC Sunday Mystery Movie*	
15	*Gunsmoke*	CBS
16	*Happy Days*	ABC
17	*Good Times*	CBS
	Barnaby Jones	
19	*Monday Night Football*	ABC
	CBS Friday Night Movie	CBS
21	*Tuesday Movie of the Week*	ABC
22	*The Streets of San Francisco*	
23	*Adam-12*	NBC
	ABC Sunday Night Movie	ABC
25	*The Rookies*	

Resolving this issue was the primary use of a number two pencil.

Christmas traditions on television.

"You're a mean one, Mr. Grinch. Your heart's an empty hole."

Sung by Thurl Ravenscroft...

who for more than 50 years was the uncredited voice of Tony the Tiger for Kellogg's Frosted Flakes. His booming bass gave the cereal's tiger mascot a voice with the catchphrase *"They're g-r-r-r-eat!!"*

You need a ticket to get in line.

Pardon Me

The House Judiciary Committee indicts President Richard Nixon for impeachment over the Watergate Scandal. In August, Nixon resigns his office, the first president to do so. Vice President Gerald Ford is sworn in as 38th president. In September, Ford grants Nixon a "full, free and absolute pardon."

Match Game '74 with the incomparable Gene Rayburn.

Stay sharp.

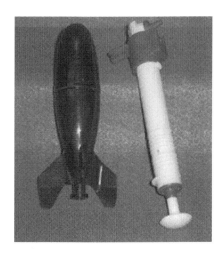

Technology. Everybody was a rocket man.

Chapter 4: Golden Skate

Just down the way from Country Earl's in Simpsonville was the Golden Skate. The roller skating rink was a main draw for the kids back then. The smell of fresh popcorn was always in the air. The music was loud and usually playing something disco oriented, most likely from *KC and the Sunshine Band*. When I was eight or nine years old, a friend had a birthday party there. It was the fastest two hours ever.

At the movies

1974 by the numbers, in no particular order...

1. The Godfather: Part II

The early life and career of Vito Corleone in 1920's New York City is portrayed, while his son, Michael, expands and tightens his grip on the family crime syndicate. *Widely considered the best movie of all time, it pretty much swept the Academy Awards that year and also launched the career of Robert De Niro who would rise to superstardom.*

2. Blazing Saddles

In order to ruin a western town, a corrupt politician appoints an African American Sheriff, who promptly becomes his most formidable adversary. *The comedy/western film made 1974 a very good year for the team of Mel Brooks and Gene Wilder.*

3. Zardoz

In the distant future, Zardoz, an unseen "God" who speaks through an idol, leads a barbaric race called the Brutals. *The science fantasy film, and later a book, was written, produced, and directed by John Boorman.*

4. Chinatown

A private detective hired to expose an adulterer finds himself caught up in a web of deceit, corruption, and murder. *The movie earned six Academy Award Nominations, including Best Actor (Jack Nicholson) and Best Actress (Faye Dunaway).*

5. Murder on the Orient Express

In December 1935, when his train is stopped by deep snow, detective Hercule Poirot is called on to solve a murder that occurred in his car the night before. *The film had six Academy Award Nominations, and won Best Supporting Actress for Ingrid Bergman.*

6. The Longest Yard

A sadistic warden asks a former pro quarterback, now serving time in his prison, to put together a team of inmates to take on the guards in this sports/comedy film. *The film was shot on location at Georgia State Prison in Reidsville, Georgia, with cooperation of then-Governor (and future president) Jimmy Carter.*

7. Thunderbolt and Lightfoot

With the help of an irreverent young sidekick, a bank robber gets his old gang back together to organize a daring new heist. *Clint Eastwood and Jeff Bridges were the backbone of this movie which earned Bridges an Academy Award Nomination for Best Supporting Actor.*

8. Young Frankenstein

An American grandson of the infamous scientist is invited to Transylvania, where he discovers the process that reanimates a dead body. *Another successful comedy from the team of Mel Brooks and Gene Wilder, two creative geniuses.*

9. The Texas Chain Saw Massacre

Two siblings and three of their friends, en route to visit their grandfather's grave in Texas, end up falling victim to a family of cannibalistic psychopaths. *The movie was banned outright in several countries, and numerous theaters later stopped showing the film in response to complaints about its violence, which was largely perpetrated with a chainsaw.*

10. Death Wish

A New York City Architect becomes a one-man vigilante squad after his wife is murdered by street punks. *Due to its support of vigilantism, it began widespread debate in America over how to deal with rampant crime.*

Honorable Mentions:

The Towering Inferno

At the opening party of a colossal, but poorly constructed, high rise office building, a massive fire breaks out that threatens to destroy the tower and everyone in it. *The action film was Nominated for eight Academy Awards, winning three, including Best Film Editing and Best Cinematography.*

Earthquake

When the big one hits Los Angeles, all hell breaks loose. *Movie theaters showed the film in "Sensurround", a new technology rolled out specifically for this movie that made the sound so loud it actually vibrated the seats.*

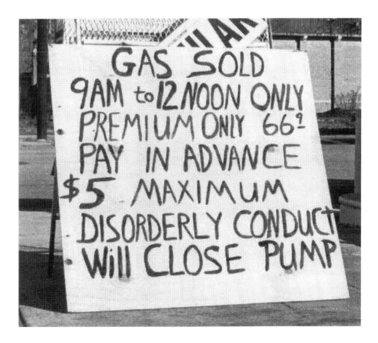

Running on Empty...

OPEC - The Organization of the Petroleum Exporting Countries (i.e. the Middle East) was founded in 1960 in Baghdad, Iraq. In 1973 their embargo of the U.S. caused a lot of headaches.

"Here's Johnny!..."

The King of Late Night TV.

Best $1 you ever spent.

Well, I used to wake the mornin'
Before the rooster crowed
Searchin' for soda bottles
To get myself some dough
Brought 'em down to the corner
Down to the country store
Cash 'em in, and give my money
To a man named Curtis Loew
--Ronnie Van Zant

From Lynyrd Skynyrd's *"The Ballad of Curtis Loew"*
On the *"Second Helping"* Album...released April 1974.

Technology meets creativity.

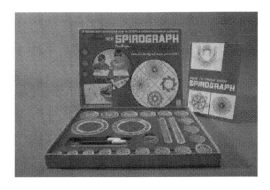

The "Viewmaster".

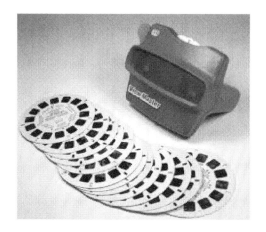

Who says?

What in the world 1974

French acrobat Philippe Petit walks across a high wire slung between the twin towers of the World Trade Center in New York.

For the ears

1974 Rock by the numbers, in no particular order...

On the Turntable
1. **Fulfillingness' First Finale** – Stevie Wonder
2. **Natty Dread** – Bob Marley and the Wailers
3. **Pretzel Logic** – Steely Dan
4. **461 Ocean Boulevard** – Eric Clapton
5. **Bad Company** – Bad Company
6. **Heart Like A Wheel** – Linda Ronstadt
7. **Second Helping** – Lynyrd Skynrd
8. **Diamond Dogs** – David Bowie
9. **It's Too Late To Stop Now** – Van Morrison
10. **What Were Once Vices Are Now Habits** – The Doobie Bros.
11. **Its Only Rock N Roll** – The Rolling Stones
12. **Before The Flood** – Bob Dylan/The Band
13. **On The Beach** – Neil Young
14. **Can't Get Enough** – Barry White
15. **Sheer Heart Attack** - Queen

On the Radio
1. **No Woman, No Cry** - Bob Marley and the Wailers
2. **Sweet Home Alabama** - Lynyrd Skynyrd
3. **You Ain't Seen Nothin' Yet** - Bachman-Turner Overdrive
4. **Rock Your Baby** - George McCrae
5. **Lady Marmalade** - LaBelle
6. **Autobahn** - Kraftwerk
7. **Help Me** - Joni Mitchell
8. **Waterloo** - Abba
9. **Can't Get Enough of Your Love, Babe** - Barry White
10. **Tell Me Something Good** - Rufus

Patty

We wondered along with our parents about Patty Hearst being kidnapped by the Symbionese Liberation Army and forced to rob banks. Was it real? Or scripted? After all, the San Francisco area had been the birthplace of many fantastic creations...including *The Grateful Dead*.

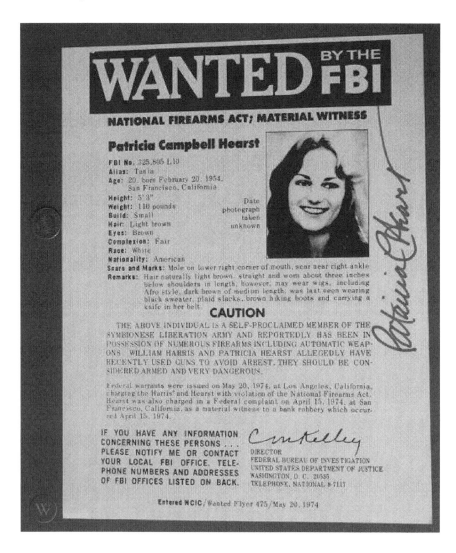

On the tube 1974

1. Little House on the Prairie (1974–1983)

The life and adventures of the Ingalls family in the nineteenth century American Midwest.

2. Happy Days (1974–1984)

The Cunningham family live through the 1950s with help and guidance from the lovable and almost superhuman greaser, Fonzie.

3. Barney Miller (1975–1982)

The Captain of the NYPD 12th Precinct and his staff handle the various local troubles and characters that come into the squad room.

4. Good Times (1974–1979)

A poor family make the best of things in the Chicago housing projects.

5. The Six Million Dollar Man (1974–1978)

After a severely injured test pilot is rebuilt with nuclear powered limbs and implants, he serves as an intelligence agent.

6. The Rockford Files (1974–1980)

The cases of an easy going ex-convict turned private investigator.

7. The Sweeney (1974–1978)

Jack Regan is a hard edged detective in the Flying Squad of London's Metropolitan Police. He pursues villains by methods which are underhanded and often illegal themselves, frequently violent and more often than not successful.

8. Shazam! (1974–1977)

A young boy, able to transform into the superhero Captain Marvel, travels the country fighting evil and helping people.

9. Land of the Lost (1974–1977)

A family is thrown back in time and must survive in a dinosaur dominated land.

10. Kolchak: The Night Stalker (1974–1975)

A newspaper reporter investigates strange supernatural occurrences in Chicago.

Honorable Mention (Tie):

Police Woman (1974–1978)

Follows Sergeant "Pepper" Anderson, LAPD's top undercover cop. A member of the Criminal Conspiracy Unit, Pepper works the wild side of the street, where she poses as everything from a gangster's moll to a streetwalker to a prison inmate.

Chico and the Man (1974–1978)

The relationship between a cranky old mechanic and a twenty-something Chicano.

The weapons of the game "Clue".

Top TV Shows of 1974   (as measured by Nielsen Media Research)

1	*All in the Family*	CBS
2	*Sanford and Son*	NBC
3	*Chico and the Man*	
4	*The Jeffersons*	
5	*M*A*S*H*	
6	*Rhoda*	
7	*Good Times*	CBS
8	*The Waltons*	
9	*Maude*	
10	*Hawaii Five-O*	
11	*The Mary Tyler Moore Show*	
12	*The Rockford Files*	NBC
13	*Little House on the Prairie*	
14	*Kojak*	CBS
15	*Police Woman*	NBC
16	*S.W.A.T.*	ABC
17	*The Bob Newhart Show*	CBS
18	*The Wonderful World of Disney*	NBC
	The Rookies	ABC
20	*Mannix*	CBS
	Cannon	
	Cher	
22	*The Streets of San Francisco*	ABC
	The NBC Sunday Mystery Movie	NBC
25	*Paul Sand in Friends and Lovers*	
	Tony Orlando & Dawn	

Chapter 5: Pong

For a mere quarter we could enjoy cutting edge technology by playing the newly invented "Pong" video game at the Arcade, or sometimes a hotel lobby. By the end of the decade, we would be playing it at home on our TV.

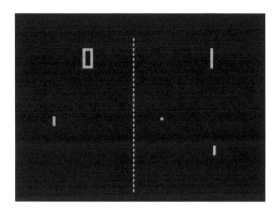

Officially: **"Pong** is one of the earliest arcade video games. It is a table tennis sports game featuring simple two-dimensional graphics. The game was originally manufactured by Atari, which released it in 1972."

Atari Home System...arcade on the couch.

8 Track Tape

The bulky box-like 8 track tape was state of the art. But if you had a favorite song you had to listen to the other stuff on the tape before it would play again. There were always infomercials on TV by companies like "K-Tel" offering greatest hits tapes you could order by mail.

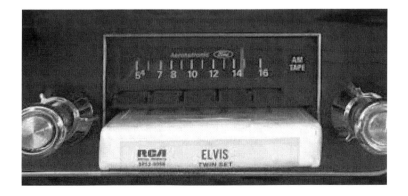

At the movies

1975 by the numbers, in no particular order…

1. Monty Python and the Holy Grail

A British comedy about King Arthur and his Knights of the Round Table. *It was conceived during the hiatus between the third and fourth seasons of their BBC Television Series, "Monty Python's Flying Circus", and illuminated the genius of cast members John Cleese and Eric Idle.*

2. One Flew Over the Cuckoo's Nest

A criminal pleads insanity, and once in the mental institution rebels against the oppressive nurse and rallies up the patients. *The film earned five Academy Awards including Best Picture, Director, Writing, Actor (Jack Nicholson), and Actress (Louise Fletcher).*

3. Jaws

When a killer shark unleashes chaos on a beach resort, it's up to a local sheriff, a marine biologist, and an old seafarer to hunt the beast down. *The film won three Oscars, including Best Music/Original Dramatic Score for John Williams, for the theme that plays every time the shark is stalking a victim.*

4. Nashville

Over the course of a few hectic days, numerous interrelated people prepare for a political convention as secrets and lies are surfaced and revealed. *The movie was Nominated for five Academy Awards, including Best Picture.*

5. The Rocky Horror Picture Show

A newly engaged couple have a breakdown in an isolated area and must pay a call to the bizarre residence of Dr. Frank-N-Furter in this musical horror comedy. *The film showcased the singing and acting talents of the rock performer Meat Loaf, and it remains a cult classic to this day.*

6. Three Days of the Condor

An intellectual CIA Researcher finds all his co-workers dead, and must outwit those responsible until he figures out who he can really trust. *Former CIA director Richard Helms acted as a personal consultant to Robert Redford for his role as The Condor.*

7. Dog Day Afternoon

A man robs a bank to pay for his lover's operation...but it evolves into a hostage situation and a media circus. *The film was Nominated for six Academy Awards, and won for Best Writing, Original Screenplay. It also demonstrated the brilliant chemistry between actors Al Pacino and John Cazale, who had just starred together the year before in "The Godfather, Part II".*

8. The Eiger Sanction

A classical art professor and collector, who doubles as a professional assassin, is coerced out of retirement to avenge the murder of an old friend. *The treacherous mountain climbing scenes further cemented Clint Eastwood's reputation as the toughest guy in Hollywood.*

9. Shampoo

An American satirical comedy-drama film set in the tumultuous year of 1968. *It won Lee Grant the Academy Award for Best*

Supporting Actress, and the soundtrack was phenomenal with music by The Beatles, Buffalo Springfield, Jefferson Airplane, Jimi Hendrix, and The Beach Boys.

10. Death Race 2000

In a dystopian future, a cross country automobile race requires contestants to run down innocent pedestrians to gain points that are tallied based on each kill's brutality. *The movie's production had many hurdles, including David Carradine having to finish his successful 'Kung Fu' TV Series before starting.*

Honorable Mentions:

Tommy

A deaf, dumb and blind boy becomes a master pinball player in this rock opera by The Who. *Band member Pete Townshend was Nominated for an Academy Award for Best Music, Original Score.*

Rollerball

Jonathan E. is the most valuable player in a corporate-controlled future violent sport known as Rollerball. *The game was so realistic that at the time of the film's release, Howard Cosell interviewed actors Norman Jewison and James Caan on "ABC's Wide World of Sports", showing clips from the film and with the two of them explaining the rules of the game.*

For the ears

1975 Rock by the numbers, in no particular order...

On the Turntable
1. **Wish You Were Here** – Pink Floyd
2. **Blood On The Tracks** – Bob Dylan
3. **Born To Run** – Bruce Springsteen

4. **A Night At The Opera** – Queen
5. **Physical Graffiti** – Led Zeppelin
6. **Horses** – Patty Smith
7. **Tonight's The Night** – Neil Young
8. **Alive!** – Kiss
9. **Toys In The Attic** – Aerosmith
10. **Live** – Bob Marley and the Wailers
11. **Welcome To My Nightmare** – Alice Cooper
12. **KC And The Sunshine Band** – KC and the Sunshine Band
13. **Young Americans** – David Bowie
14. **One Of These Nights** – The Eagles
15. **Captain Fantastic & The Brown Dirt Cowboy** – Elton John

Plenty of capers were pulled in this convenience store that was later known as "The Pantry".

In the 70's, candy was out of this world.

On the Radio
1. **Born to Run** - Bruce Springsteen
2. **Bohemian Rhapsody** - Queen
3. **Walk This Way** - Aerosmith
4. **Kashmir** - Led Zeppelin
5. **Tangled Up in Blue** - Bob Dylan
6. **Wish You Were Here** - Pink Floyd
7. **Thunder Road** - Bruce Springsteen
8. **One of These Nights** - Eagles
9. **Low Rider** - War
10. **I'm Not in Love** - 10cc

What in the world 1975

North Vietnamese enter Saigon. The last group of Americans are evacuated by helicopter at the last minute from the roof of the embassy. The War in Vietnam is over.

"Mr. Bill" was constantly in jeopardy of losing life and limb on Saturday Night Live.

Texting in the 70's.

A best seller in comic books turned out to be a kind of miniscule shrimp.

Banned by the little league football coach due to a by-product of broken bones.

On the tube 1975

1. Saturday Night Live (1975–)

A famous guest host stars in parodies and sketches created by the cast of this witty show.

2. Wonder Woman (1975–1979)

The adventures of the greatest of the female superheroes.

3. The Jeffersons (1975–1985)

A nouveau riche, African-American family who move into a luxury apartment building develop close, if occasionally fractious, relationships with other tenants.

4. Space: 1999 (1975–1977)

The crew of Moonbase Alpha must struggle to survive when a massive explosion throws the Moon from orbit into deep space.

5. Fawlty Towers (1975–1979)

Hotel owner Basil Fawlty's incompetence, short fuse, and arrogance form a combination that ensures accidents and trouble are never far away.

6. One Day at a Time (1975–1984)

The misadventures of a divorced mother, her family, and their building superintendent in Indianapolis.

7. Baretta (1975–1978)

Cases of gritty undercover New York City detective Tony B.

8. Welcome Back, Kotter (1975–1979)

A compassionate teacher returns to his inner city high school of his youth to teach a new generation of trouble making kids.

9. Starsky and Hutch (1975–1979)

Two streetwise cops bust criminals in their red-and-white Ford Torino, with the help of police snitch, Huggy Bear.

10. S.W.A.T. (1975–1976)

The missions of a major city's police department's Special Weapons and Tactics unit.

Honorable Mention:

Austin City Limits (1975–)

Established singer-songwriters and acclaimed newcomers perform country, blues, rock, folk, bluegrass, and related styles of music from Studio 6A of public television station KLRU (formerly KLRN) at the University of Texas at Austin.

The squeeze police.

Top TV Shows of 1975 (as measured by Nielsen Media Research)

1	*All in the Family*	CBS
2	*Rich Man, Poor Man*	ABC
3	*Laverne & Shirley*	
4	*Maude*	CBS
5	*The Bionic Woman*	ABC
6	*Phyllis*	CBS
7	*Sanford and Son*	NBC
	Rhoda	CBS
9	*The Six Million Dollar Man*	
10	*ABC Monday Night Movie*	ABC
11	*Happy Days*	
12	*One Day at a Time*	CBS
13	*ABC Sunday Night Movie*	ABC
14	*The Waltons*	CBS
	*M*A*S*H*	
16	*Starsky & Hutch*	
	Good Heavens	ABC
18	*Welcome Back, Kotter*	
19	*The Mary Tyler Moore Show*	
20	*Kojak*	CBS
21	*The Jeffersons*	
22	*Baretta*	ABC
23	*The Sonny & Cher Show*	CBS
24	*Good Times*	
25	*Chico and the Man*	NBC

Bert and Ernie...the original Beavis and Butthead.

What in the world 1975

Bill Gates and Paul Allen found the Microsoft corporation. The Altair becomes the first widely available personal computer running Microsoft's BASIC software.

Their hearty home-style cooking arrived on scene in 1975.

Bionic

Pretending to be bionic just like the "Six Million Dollar Man", Steve Austin...even making the bionic sound effects we heard on TV.

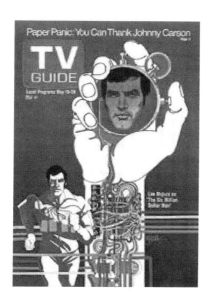

Sold at Wholesale Enterprises on Highway 14

Bottle rockets $2.50 for 72. Bottle rocket wars...priceless.

Record Player

Pressed vinyl. A turntable with a delicate needle. Albums and "45" singles. This is the way music was dispensed to the ears.

Oscar the grouch...the precursor to living in a van down by the river.

At the movies

1976 by the numbers, in no particular order...

1. A Star Is Born

A has-been rock star falls in love with a young, up-and-coming songstress. *The film won the Academy Award for Best Music, Original Song, for the duo of actress/singer Barbra Streisand and lyrics writer Paul Williams.*

2. Taxi Driver

Mentally unstable Travis works as an overnight shift taxi driver in New York City, where perceived decadence and sleaze fuels his urge for violence. *The movie earned four Academy Award Nominations, including Best Picture, Actor (Robert De Niro), and Actress for Jodie Foster, who was only 13 years old at the time.*

3. Rocky

Small-time boxer, and part time street thug, Rocky Balboa gets a chance to fight a heavyweight champion as part of the celebration of the bicentennial year. *The film was Nominated for ten Academy Awards, and among the three wins was Best Picture. Sylvester Stallone both wrote and starred in the movie, following in the footsteps of acting greats Charlie Chaplain and Orson Welles as the only ones to accomplish this feat.*

4. Carrie

Carrie White is a shy, friendless, and strange teenage girl who unleashes her telekinetic powers after being humiliated by her classmates at her senior prom. *This supernatural horror thriller was adapted from creative genius Stephen King's novel and helped* launch the careers of Sissy Spacek and John Travolta.

5. The Outlaw Josey Wales

A Missouri farmer joins a Confederate Guerrilla Unit to get revenge on the Union soldiers who murdered his family. *Another successful classic featuring both the directing and acting skills of Clint Eastwood.*

6. The Shootist

A terminally ill gunfighter spends his last days looking for a way to die with minimum pain and maximum dignity. *This was the final film for the great John Wayne, a heavy smoker, who would ironically die from cancer just a couple of years later.*

7. All the President's Men

"The Washington Post" reporters Bob Woodward and Carl Bernstein uncover the details of the Watergate scandal that leads to President Richard Nixon's resignation. *The movie earned eight Academy Award Nominations, and the team of Robert Redford and Dustin Hoffman as the principal characters was superb.*

8. Logan's Run

Anybody over 30 must be eliminated and Logan is one to enforce it, until he turns of age and goes on the run. *The film won a Special Academy Award for Visual Effects and helped launch the career of Michael York.*

9. King Kong

An exploration for oil comes to an isolated island and encounters a colossal giant gorilla in this remake of the 1933 black and white film. *Of the three King Kong films, it is the only one to feature the World Trade Center instead of the Empire State Building.*

10. Network

Unstable television news anchor Howard Beale, who is "mad as hell", is exploited to boost failing viewership of the network. *The film garnered ten Academy Award Nominations and provided wins for Best Actor (Peter Finch) and Best Actress (Faye Dunaway).*

Honorable Mentions:

The Bad News Bears

Walter Matthau plays an aging, down-on-his-luck, ex-minor leaguer who coaches a team of misfits in baseball and in life. *"Saturday Night Live" did a parody of the film when Matthau guest hosted, called "The Bad News Bees", in which John Belushi and Dan Aykroyd donned their bee costumes (the "King Bee" skit) for what would be the final time before Belushi's untimely death.*

The Omen

A series of mysterious and gruesome deaths around a child finally enlightens others that he is indeed the Antichrist. *Brilliantly acted by all involved, the film won the Academy Award for Best Music/Original Score for the intense and creepy background tracks.*

What in the world 1976

The Viking 2 spacecraft lands on Mars.

1976 Olympic Gold Medalist and American Hero Bruce Jenner.

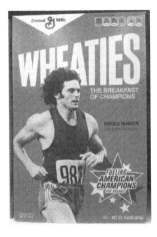

You know how the story ended.

For the ears

1976 Rock by the numbers, in no particular order...

On the Turntable
1. **Songs In The Key Of Life** – Stevie Wonder
2. **Station To Station** – David Bowie
3. **Ramones** – Ramones
4. **Hotel California** – The Eagles
5. **Boston** – Boston
6. **2112** – Rush
7. **Desire** – Bob Dylan
8. **Frampton Comes Alive** – Peter Frampton
9. **Night Moves** – Bob Seger
10. **Dreamboat Annie** – Heart
11. **One More From The Road** – Lynyrd Skynyrd

12. **Fly Like An Eagle** – The Steve Miller Band
13. **Black And Blue** – The Rolling Stones
14. **Takin' It To The Streets** – The Doobie Brothers
15. **Silk Degrees** – Boz Scaggs

News was actually printed on paper.

On the Radio
1. **Hotel California** - The Eagles
2. **Go Your Own Way** - Fleetwood Mac
3. **More Than a Feeling** - Boston
4. **Anarchy in the UK** - The Sex Pistols
5. **Dancing Queen** - Abba
6. **(Don't Fear) The Reaper** - Blue Oyster Cult
7. **Night Moves** - Bob Seger
8. **Blitzkrieg Bop** - The Ramones
9. **The Boys Are Back in Town** - Thin Lizzy
10. **Play That Funky Music** - Wild Cherry

On the tube 1976

1. Charlie's Angels (1976–1981)

Television series about a wealthy mystery man who runs a detective agency via a speakerphone and his personal assistant, John Bosley. His detectives are three beautiful women.

2. Three's Company (1976–1984)

The misadventures of two women and one man living in one apartment and their neighbors.

3. Alice (1976–1985)

The misadventures and trials of an aspiring singer and her co-workers at a greasy spoon diner.

4. Laverne & Shirley (1976–1983)

The misadventures of two single women in the 1950's and 60's.

5. Black Sheep Squadron (1976–1978)

The dramatized World War II adventures of U.S. Major Gregory "Pappy" Boyington and his U.S. Marine Attack Squadron 214, (The Black Sheep Squadron).

6. The Bionic Woman (1976–1978)

After fully recovering from her nearly fatal bout of bionic rejection, Jamie Sommers, the first female cyborg, is assigned to spy missions of her own.

7. Quincy M.E. (1976–1983)

The cases of a coroner who investigates suspicious deaths that usually suggest murder.

8. How the West Was Won (1976–)

The Macahans, a family from Virginia, headed by Zeb Macahan, travel across the country to pioneer a new land and a new home in the American West.

9. The Muppet Show (1976–1981)

Kermit the Frog and his friends put on a weekly variety show.

10. What's Happening!! (1976–1979)

A trio of black youths learn about life, love, friendship, credit cards, gambling, and a variety of other things while growing up in an inner city.

Honorable Mention:

The Gong Show (1976–1980)

Zany amateur talent contest judged by three celebrities, and hosted by the loveable Chuck (em)Barriss and his sidekick *"Gene Gene the Dance Machine"*.

The "Unknown Comic" from the Gong Show.

Kermit knew the old spice cologne would work.

Standard compliment from Fred G. Sanford.

The candy bar that went on forever had a ruler on the wrapper.

President Carter's brother was famous too.

Top TV Shows of 1976   (as measured by Nielsen Media Research)

1	Happy Days	
2	Laverne & Shirley	ABC
3	ABC Monday Night Movie	
4	M*A*S*H	CBS
5	Charlie's Angels	ABC
6	The Big Event	NBC
7	The Six Million Dollar Man	
	ABC Sunday Night Movie	ABC
8	Baretta	
	One Day at a Time	CBS
11	Three's Company	ABC
12	All in the Family	CBS
13	Welcome Back, Kotter	ABC
14	The Bionic Woman	
15	The Waltons	CBS
	Little House on the Prairie	NBC
17	Barney Miller	ABC
18	60 Minutes	CBS
	Hawaii Five-O	
20	NBC Monday Night Movie	NBC
21	Rich Man, Poor Man Book II	
22	Monday Night Football	ABC
23	Eight Is Enough	
24	The Jeffersons	CBS
25	What's Happening!!	ABC

The main music on the record player in the lodge at Eagle's Nest Camp.

Hey Snowman, you got your ears on?

Spanning the globe to bring you the constant variety of sport. The thrill of victory...and the agony of defeat. The human drama of athletic competition.

What in the world 1976

Apple Computer is founded by Steve Jobs and Stephen Wozniak.

Crank Call

The telephone was one of those tethered models. Very primitive. But you could crank call people and get away with it. There was no caller I.D. There was no call return. The callee was helpless as the pranksters enjoyed total anonymity. Of course, we never did anything like that.

Five Oh

Kam Fong as Chin Ho. Or was it the other way around? The show was a fan favorite with supercop Jack McGarrett, his jet black Cadillac, and tag phrase *"Book 'em Danno"*.

Chapter 6: The Freedom Train

Tickets were $2 for adults and $1 for children when *"The Freedom Train"* pulled in to Greenville S.C. on November 3, 1976. And this child was able to celebrate the bicentennial year in style. The whole family went to see the deal. Everybody put a bicentennial quarter on the train track for the train to run over to keep as a souvenir. America was a great place to live, but I had no idea how hard our forefathers worked to get it to this point.

This 26-car train was powered by three newly restored steam locomotives. The viewing train itself consisted of 10 display cars, converted from baggage cars. They carried more than 500 treasures of Americana, including:

George Washington's copy of *The Constitution*
The original *Louisiana Purchase*

Judy Garland's dress from *The Wizard of Oz*
Joe Frazier's boxing trunks
Dr. Martin Luther King's *"I have a dream"* speech
Lewis and Clark's map
Replicas of Jesse Owens' four Olympic gold medals from 1936
Hank Aaron's "714" bat
Jim Bowie's knife
President Kennedy's handwritten inaugural speech
Tools from the gold miners of 1849
Lincoln's stovepipe hat
A rock from the Moon
Thomas Edison's first working light bulb
NBA star Bob Lanier's size-20 sneakers
    ... and even Ben Franklin's *Poor Richard's Almanac*,
        first published in 1782.
  It was *"for conveying instruction among the common people"*.

All decked out in red white and blue as a colorful celebration of America's past, the train's tour of all 48 contiguous states lasted from April 1, 1975, until December 31, 1976. More than 7 million Americans visited the train during its tour, while millions more stood trackside to see it go by.

Car #1 THE BEGINNING: A look at the first moments of the struggle for independence from 18th century New England. Visitors will view an exhibit that includes precious documents that are the foundation of our liberty, such as George Washington's copy of the Constitution and Pennsylvania's Ratification of the Constitution.

Car #2 EXPLORATION AND EXPANSION: An exhibit of American frontiers from the opening of the west to the penetration of space. Early pioneers were lured by gold; modern pioneers are lured by the mysteries of outer space.

Car #3 GROWTH OF THE NATION: Changes wrought on this country as cities, farms, transportation centers and energy production have been added to the early landscape. America the Beautiful provides a musical reminder of the need for preserving our National environment.

Car #4 ORIGINS: Tracing the ethnic, religious and geographical origins of contemporary Americans. The music of dozens of lands speaks of this unique land of opportunity.

Car #5 INNOVATIONS: A review of the inventors and technicians whose efforts are synonymous with "American know-how" and the development of our free enterprise system and the American we know today. Patent drawings and models of inventions big and small are displayed.

Car #6 LABOR AND PROFESSIONS: An examination of the diversity and magnitude of fields of creative Americans and the products of their work. The pursuits of Americans, from silversmiths and glassblowers to film makers and scientists, are outlined.

Car #7 SPORTS: A panorama of the sporting American as hero, participant, and spectator. Scenes, artifacts and film clips from a sports-loving country include a sprinting Jesse Owens, Secretariat romping to victory, and Babe Ruth batting a home run.

Car #8 PERFORMING ARTS: A montage of American talent through vaudeville, Hollywood, radio and television, and the Broadway stage. The sounds of entertainment, from television to vaudeville, provide a musical backdrop for this dramatic part of America.

Car #9 FINE ARTS: A gallery of American painting and sculpture reflecting the evolution of American society. Priceless paintings and sculpture will capture the look of our country from 18th century portraiture through sweeping western landscapes.

Car #10 CONFLICT AND RESOLUTION: A dramatic portrayal of five events in American history which have tested the fiber of our system but from which Americans have emerged stronger and more unified. President Lincoln's assassination and President Roosevelt's economic strife will help portray the ability of a people to grow.

The Conehead family from "Saturday Night Live".

"Ho Jo's" had the best fried clams in Greenville.

Astronaut approved drink mix complete with toy Lunar Rover.

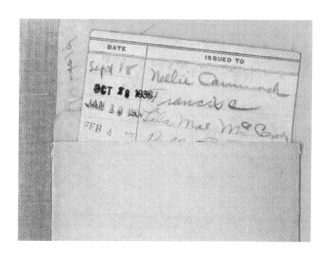

The librarian required a signature at checkout.

*The sign at the counter said "In God We Trust...all others pay cash".
Laurel and Hardy silent movies were on the screen
and 1970's music was in the air.*

What in the world 1977

"Star Wars" is released, to the delight of millions.

*1977 was a big year for Hertz Rent-A-Car ads...
and their pitchman at the time, O.J. Simpson.*

Chapter 7: The Kang

It was a hot August afternoon in rural South Carolina. I was in the car with my mother driving. I forget where we were going. A man on the radio said "The Kang is dead". I asked, "Mom, who is the Kang?." Through her tears she replied, "Elvis Pressley, the King of Rock and Roll". At just 42, he was gone way too soon...but his music will live on forever.

What in the world 1977

A nuclear proliferation pact that curbs the spread of nuclear weapons is signed by 15 countries, including the U.S. and USSR.

Standard breakfast fare.

Endorsed by "Milton the Toaster".

Developing Film

Our cameras used film. Even the fancy video cameras the TV crews used. That's where their famous tag line *"Film at Eleven"* evolved from. For our families it was common to take a roll or three of film to the drug store to get the pictures developed. Go back about a week later to pick them up. You never knew what you had until you opened up the envelope to view them. There would always be one in the bunch that had the camera operator's finger errantly in the shot.

Augusta

In 1977 Grandpa got us tickets to The Masters. The grass was wet and slippery that Sunday. As we walked right in front of a live TV camera, and with thousands of other golf fans around us, Uncle Bill slipped and fell, soiling his khaki pants with mud and grass. Not wanting to be caught up in the embarrassment, me and Grandpa pretended not to know him and quickly walked the other way. When he finally caught up, Billy cussed us all the way to the second fairway.

At the movies

1977 by the numbers, in no particular order...

1. Star Wars: Episode IV - A New Hope (The Original Star Wars Movie)

Fighter pilot Luke Skywalker joins forces with a cast of characters to save the galaxy from the Empire's world-destroying death star ray gun, while also attempting to rescue Princess Leia from impending doom. *The film won six Academy Awards, besting in Set Decoration, Costume Design, Sound, Editing, Visual Effects, and Original Music Score.*

2. The Deep

Two scuba divers come across underwater treasure in the form of drugs and are in grave danger from the bad guys who want it. *Another hit movie based on a book by writer Peter Benchley of "Jaws" fame.*

3. Smokey and the Bandit

The Bandit (Burt Reynolds) is hired to run a tractor trailer full of beer over state lines, while in hot pursuit by a pesky sheriff. *Supporting Actor Jerry Reed's "Eastbound and Down" song became a hit on the Country Music Charts, ending up number two.*

4. Close Encounters of the Third Kind

Richard Dreyfuss stars as Roy Neary, a blue-collar worker in Indiana, whose life changes after an encounter with a UFO. *The film was Nominated for nine Academy Awards, winning for Best Cinematography and Best Sound Effects Editing, and furthering the impressive career of director Steven Spielberg.*

5. A Bridge Too Far

During "Operation Market Garden" in WW II, the Allies attempt to capture several strategically important bridges in the Netherlands in the hope of breaking the German lines. *The ensemble cast was a who's who of actors at the time, including James Caan, Michael Caine, Sean Connery, Edward Fox, Elliott Gould, Gene Hackman, Anthony Hopkins, Laurence Olivier, Ryan O'Neal, Robert Redford, and Maximilian Schell.*

6. Saturday Night Fever

Teenage Brooklyn paint salesman Tony Minero escapes the harsh reality of his bleak family life by dominating the dance floor at the local disco. *The movie's music fueled the Disco Craze of the time and it remains the best-selling soundtrack ever with over 54 million units sold as of 2019.*

7. Annie Hall

Neurotic New York comedian Alvy Singer falls in love with the ditzy Annie Hall. *The film won four Academy Awards, including*

Best Director and Best Writing for Woody Allen, and Best Actress for Diane Keaton.

8. Eraserhead

A horror cult classic, filmed in black and white, has Henry Spencer trying to survive his insane surroundings. *Famed Director Stanley Kubrick said this was his favorite film and that it served as an influence on his 1980 movie "The Shining".*

9. The Car

A small desert town is terrorized by a seemingly possessed car intent on causing destruction and death. *The "evil" black car in the film was a highly customized 1971 Lincoln Continental Mark III, designed by famed Hollywood car customizer George Barris.*

10. The Spy Who Loved Me

James Bond investigates the hijacking of British and Russian submarines carrying nuclear warheads, with the help of a K.G.B. Agent, whose lover he killed. *The theme song, "Nobody Does It Better", was performed by Carly Simon and became a smash hit, making it all the way to number two on the US Billboard Hot 100 Chart.*

Honorable Mention:

Slap Shot

A failing ice hockey team finds success with outrageously violent goonery in this sports comedy. *Paul Newman stated that the most fun he ever had making a movie was on "Slap Shot", as he had played the sport while young and was fascinated by the real players around him.*

The cast of "Star Wars" in 1977...Han Solo, Darth Vader, Chewbacca, Princess Leia, Luke Skywalker, and R2D2.

For the ears

1977 Rock by the numbers, in no particular order...

On the Turntable
1. **Rumours** – Fleetwood Mac
2. **Animals** – Pink Floyd
3. **Aja** – Steely Dan
4. **Heroes** – David Bowie
5. **Exodus** – Bob Marley and the Wailers
6. **Saturday Night Fever** – The Bee Gees (& Others)
7. **Terrapin Station** – The Grateful Dead
8. **Bat Out Of Hell** – Meat Loaf
9. **Rocket To Russia** – Ramones
10. **Love Gun** – Kiss
11. **Street Survivors** – Lynyrd Skynyrd
12. **The Grand Illusion** – Styx
13. **CSN** – Crosby, Stills, & Nash

14. **Slowhand** – Eric Clapton
15. **Cat Scratch Fever** – Ted Nugent

Don't look Ethel...

On the Radio
1. **Stayin' Alive** - The Bee Gees
2. **We Will Rock You/We Are the Champions** - Queen
Gr4. **Best of My Love** - The Emotions
5. **God Save the Queen** - The Sex Pistols
6. **Brick House** - The Commodores
7. **Dreams** - Fleetwood Mac
8. **Paradise by the Dashboard Light** - Meat Loaf
9. **I Feel Love** - Donna Summer
10. **Jamming** - Bob Marley and the Wailers

Greenville Memorial Auditorium.

Flair Tops McDaniel

Ric Flair defeated Wahoo McDaniel in the main event Monday night of Mid-Atlantic wrestling at the Auditorium.

In a tag team match, Ronnie Garvin and Tiger Conway, Jr., defeated the Monguls. Johnny Eagle beat Bill White, Steve Bolus triumphed over Two-Ton Harris, and Vic Rosettani defeated Angelo Poffo.

Sky City was a hub of activity in Mauldin, South Carolina.

On the tube 1977

1. CHiPs (1977–1983)

The adventures of two California Highway Patrol motorcycle officers.

2. The Love Boat (1977–1987)

The romantic and comic tales of the passengers and crew of the cruise ship, Pacific Princess.

3. The Incredible Hulk (1978–1982)

A fugitive scientist has the curse of becoming a powerful green monster under extreme emotional stress.

4. Soap (1977–1981)

The soap-operish antics of two families: the Campbells and the Tates.

5. Fantasy Island (1977–1984)

Accounts of visitors to a unique resort island in the Pacific Ocean that can fulfill literally any fantasy requested, but rarely turn out as expected.

6. The Professionals (1977–1983)

Bodie and Doyle, top agents for Britain's CI5 (Criminal Intelligence 5), and their controller, George Cowley fight terrorism and similar high-profile crimes.

7. Eight Is Enough (1977–1981)

This comedy drama focused on a family with eight very independent children.

8. Mind Your Language (1977–1986)

Jeremy Brown is a put-upon language teacher who tries to make a living by teaching English to immigrants. With pupils from India, France, China, and many other countries.

9. Man from Atlantis (1977–1978)

The adventures of a man with amphibious abilities.

10. The Amazing Spider-Man (1977–1979)

With the powers given by the bite of a radioactive spider, a young man fights crime as a wall-crawling superhero.

Honorable Mention:

Lou Grant (1977–1982)

The trials of a former television station manager, turned newspaper city editor, and his journalist staff.

Mid Atlantic Wrestling every Saturday morning.

Jimmy slowed down more than the economy in the late 70's.

Hall's Barber Shop. The patriarch, Bascomb Hall, sold hot peppers here...and occasionally gave Mohawk haircuts to Mauldin High Athletes.

Chapter 8: Skynyrd

The iconic southern rock band Lynyrd Skynyrd played their last concert at the Greenville Memorial Auditorium on October 12, 1977. Several members of the band, including founder and lead singer Ronnie Van Zant, died when their plane crashed into a swamp in rural Mississippi en route to their next show, which was to be held in Baton Rouge, Louisiana. Our favorite song then is our favorite song now: *"Tuesday's Gone with the Wind."*

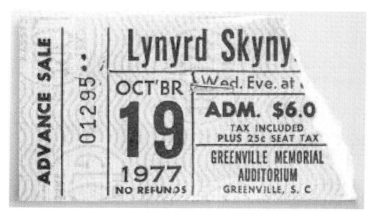

Top TV Shows of 1977   (as measured by Nielsen Media Research)

1 Laverne & Shirley
2 Happy Days   ABC
3 Three's Company
   60 Minutes   CBS
4 Charlie's Angels   ABC
   All in the Family   CBS
7 Little House on the Prairie NBC
8 Alice
   M*A*S*H   CBS
10 One Day at a Time
11 How the West Was Won
12 Eight Is Enough
                                           ABC
13 Soap
14 The Love Boat
15 NBC Monday Night Movie NBC
16 Monday Night Football
   Fantasy Island   ABC
17
   Barney Miller
19 Project U.F.O.   NBC
   ABC Sunday Night Movie ABC
20
   The Waltons
22 Barnaby Jones   CBS
23 Hawaii Five-O
24 ABC Monday Night Movie ABC
25 Rhoda   CBS

Drive In

The Drive-In Theater was a big deal in the 70's. We packed up the family in the station wagon and would open the hatchback for the kids to sit on and set out lawn chairs for the grown-ups. The sound was provided by an individual speaker that we could put in the car or leave next to it. When the movie *"Grease"* came out, we first saw it at the Drive In.

At the movies

1978 by the numbers, in no particular order...

1. Animal House

At a 1962 college, Dean Wormer is determined to expel the entire Delta Tau Chi Fraternity, but those troublemakers have other plans for him. *Actor John Belushi was stellar as Bluto Blutarski in this uproarious comedy.*

2. Grease

Good girl Sandy and greaser Danny fell in love over the summer, but can they keep their relationship when being cool in high school causes problems. *The film earned an Academy Award Nomination for best song, as Olivia Newton-John sang "Hopelessly Devoted To You".*

3. Halloween

Fifteen years after murdering his sister on Halloween night 1963, Michael Myers escapes from a mental hospital and returns to the small town of Haddonfield, Illinois to kill again. *John Carpenter's brilliant screenplay and direction helped launch the career of Jamie Lee Curtis.*

4. Watership Down

A group of rabbits flee their doomed warren and face many dangers to find and protect their new home. *The animated feature has elements of horror and sadness, as it displays consequences of humans expanding their geographical footprint into nature.*

5. The Deer Hunter

Three friends from a small town in Pennsylvania experience the horror of war, both during their service in Vietnam and after they return. *The blockbuster movie was Nominated for nine Academy Awards, winning Best Picture, Best Supporting Actor (Christopher Walken), Best Director, Best Sound, and Best Editing.*

6. Jaws 2

Police Chief Brody faces another monstrous shark that is threatening the Amity Island vacationer's paradise. *The later film "Somewhere in Time" (1980) was made because Universal Pictures owed director Jeannot Szwarc a favor, since "Jaws 2" had been the studio's biggest box-office performer of 1978.*

7. Superman

An alien orphan is sent from his dying planet to Earth, where he grows up to become his adoptive home's first and greatest superhero. *Upon viewing the footage of Krypton, Warner Brothers decided to distribute not only in the U.S., but also in foreign countries.*

8. Convoy

Truckers form a mile long convoy in support of a trucker's vendetta with an abusive sheriff, based on the country song of same title by C.W. McCall. *This movie showed the CB Radio craze of the late 70's, along with the lingo that was transmitted on it.*

9. Every Which Way But Loose

California trucker turned prize-fighter Philo Beddoe (Clint Eastwood) and his pet orangutan Clyde square off with a bumbling motorcycle gang. *Many of the bad guys had appeared in Eastwood's Western movies earlier in the decade.*

10. Midnight Express

Billy Hayes, an American college student, is caught smuggling hash out of Turkey and experiences the horror of Middle East prison life. *The film garnered six Academy Award Nominations, and won for Best Writing, Screenplay Based on Material from Another Medium (Oliver Stone) and Best Music, Original Score.*

Honorable Mentions:

Heaven Can Wait

A Los Angeles Rams quarterback, accidentally taken away from his body by an overanxious angel before he was meant to die, returns to life in the body of a recently murdered millionaire. *This comedy was Nominated for nine Academy Awards, including Best Picture, Best Actor, Best Director, and Best Writer – all for Warren Beatty.*

Coming Home

A woman whose husband is fighting in Viet Nam falls in love with another man who suffered a paralyzing combat injury there. *Jon Voight (Best Actor) and Jane Fonda (Best Actress) were Oscar winners for their portrayals of two unlikely lovers.*

What in the world 1978

The world's first test-tube baby is born.

He dared you to knock this off.

For the ears

1978 Rock by the numbers, in no particular order...

On the Turntable
1. **Van Halen** – Van Halen
2. **Parallel Lines** – Blondie
3. **The Cars** – The Cars
4. **Some Girls** – The Rolling Stones
5. **Shakedown Street** – The Grateful Dead
6. **Cheap Trick At Budokan** – Cheap Trick
7. **Dire Straits** – Dire Straits
8. **Outlandos d'Amour** – The Police
9. **Waiting For Columbus** – Little Feat
10. **Double Vision** – Foreigner
11. **Some Enchanted Evening** – Blue Oyster Cult
12. **Don't Look Back** – Boston
13. **Who Are You** – The Who
14. **Comes A Time** – Neil Young
15. **Darkness On The Edge Of Town** – Bruce Springsteen

His "9 Lives" on television ended in 1978.

On the Radio
1. **I Will Survive** - Gloria Gaynor
2. **Roxanne** - The Police
3. **Sultans of Swing** - Dire Straits
4. **Heart of Glass** - Blondie
5. **One Nation Under a Groove** - Funkadelic
6. **I Wanna Be Sedated** - The Ramones
7. **Miss You** - The Rolling Stones
8. **Le Freak** - Chic
9. **Old Time Rock and Roll** - Bob Seger
10. **Rock Lobster** - The B-52's

Memes were putty silly.

On the tube 1978

1. Dallas (1978–1991)

J.R. Ewing, a Texas oil baron, uses manipulation and blackmail to achieve his ambitions, both business and personal. He often comes into conflict with his brother Bobby, his arch-enemy Cliff Barnes and his long-suffering wife Sue Ellen.

2. WKRP in Cincinnati (1978–1982)

The misadventures of the staff of a struggling Top 40 rock radio station in Cincinnati, Ohio.

3. Battlestar Galactica (1978–1979)

After the destruction of the Twelve Colonies of Mankind, the last major fighter carrier leads a makeshift fugitive fleet on a desperate search for the legendary planet Earth.

4. Taxi (1978–1983)

The staff of a New York City taxicab company go about their job while they dream of greater things.

5. Diff'rent Strokes (1978–1986)

The misadventures of a wealthy Manhattan family who adopted the children of their late African American housekeeper from Harlem.

6. Project U.F.O. (1978–1979)

Two agents of the U.S. Government's "Project Blue Book" investigate sightings of unidentified flying objects.

7. Blake's 7 (1978–1981)

A group of convicts and outcasts fight a guerrilla war against the totalitarian Terran Federation from a highly advanced alien spaceship.

8. Mork & Mindy (1978–1982)

A wacky alien comes to Earth to study its residents and the life of the human woman he boards with is never the same.

9. Grange Hill (1978–2008)

The long running television series of the Grange Hill Comprehensive School, and the children's everyday lives.

10. All Creatures Great and Small (1978–1990)

The trials and misadventures of the staff of a country veterinary office in 1940's Yorkshire.

Honorable Mention (Tie):

Vega$ (1978–1981)

Dan Tanna is a private investigator in the gambling town of Las Vegas, Nevada. Vegas can be seedy or glamorous, depending upon the point of view.

The White Shadow (1978–1981)

A white former NBA professional retires from the pro game and gets a job as a basketball coach in a predominantly black inner-city high school.

A digital watch was the closest thing to a smart phone.

Once, the cow disappeared from the roof of the store and wound up at a pep rally for the Mauldin Mavericks football team.
No one knows the details.

Spoke loudly...
The de facto result was to replicate the sound of a motorbike.

Top TV Shows of 1978 (as measured by Nielsen Media Research)

1	*Laverne & Shirley*	
2	*Three's Company*	
3	*Mork & Mindy*	ABC
	Happy Days	
5	*Angie*	
6	*60 Minutes*	CBS
7	*M*A*S*H*	
8	*The Ropers*	ABC
9	*All in the Family*	CBS
	Taxi	
11	*Eight Is Enough*	ABC
12	*Charlie's Angels*	
13	*Alice*	CBS
14	*Little House on the Prairie*	NBC
15	*ABC Sunday Night Movie*	
	Barney Miller	ABC
17	*The Love Boat*	
18	*One Day at a Time*	CBS
19	*Soap*	ABC
20	*The Dukes of Hazzard*	CBS
21	*NBC Monday Night Movie*	NBC
22	*Fantasy Island*	ABC
23	*Vega$*	
24	*Barnaby Jones*	CBS
25	*CHiPs*	NBC

> **What in the world 1978**
>
> Egypt's president Anwar Sadat and Israeli premier Menachem Begin sign a "Framework for Peace" after meeting for 13 days with Jimmy Carter at Camp David. Later they win the Nobel Peace Prize.

Chapter 9: Radar Gun

A nearby police department didn't have the budget for a state of the art radar speeding gun. So they took an old hand held hair dryer, wrapped black electrical tape around it, parked their car in the center median, and pointed it at oncoming cars. The speeders did two things after that. They hit the brakes in panicky fashion and then went to the place they bought their radar detector from and complained that it wasn't picking up the signal.

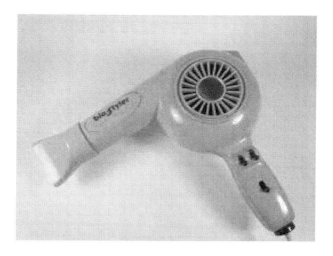

At the movies

1979 by the numbers, in no particular order...

1. Apocalypse Now

During the Vietnam War, Captain Willard is sent on a dangerous mission into Cambodia to terminate a commanding officer who went rogue. *The film was Nominated for eight Academy Awards, including Best Picture and Best Director (Francis Ford Coppola), and won for both Sound and Cinematography.*

2. Alien

After a space merchant vessel perceives an unknown transmission as a distress call, its landing on the source moon finds one of the crew attacked by a mysterious lifeform, and they soon realize that its life cycle has merely begun. *The Sci-Fi hit won the Academy Award for Best Visual Effects and launched the career of versatile actress Sigourney Weaver.*

3. Caligula

Details the graphic and shocking, yet undeniably tragic story of Rome's most infamous Caesar, Gaius Germanicus Caligula. *Under the supervision of Costume Designer Danilo Donati, three thousand five hundred ninety-two costumes were designed.*

4. Life of Brian

Born on Christmas in the stable next door to Jesus, Brian of Nazareth spends his life being mistaken for a messiah. *Another hit comedy for the British duo of John Cleese and Eric Idle of "Monty Python" fame.*

5. Mad Max

In a dystopian, rural Australia, a vengeful policeman gets even with a violent motorcycle gang who murdered his wife, his child, and his best friend. *The film helped launch the career of Mel Gibson, who would emerge as a top tier actor, producer, and director.*

6. Hair

A country boy from Oklahoma, with a destination of joining the US Army en route to Vietnam, is embraced by a group of free spirited hippies. *This hit movie, based on the cult Broadway musical of the 60's, had an outstanding soundtrack that included songs performed by some of the film's main actors.*

7. The Warriors

A scrappy New York City street gang makes their way back to home turf on Coney Island after they are framed for a murder. *According to the film's composer Barry De Vorzon, the picture was the first movie to feature an entire music score of synthesized rock 'n' roll music.*

8. Escape from Alcatraz

Clint Eastwood is outstanding as usual in this movie which is based on the true story of three inmates who, presumably, make their way to freedom from the escape-proof prison in San Francisco Bay known as "The Rock". *To this very day, the fate and/or freedom of Frank Morris and brothers John and Clarence Anglin remains a mystery.*

9. Rocky II

Rocky struggles in family life after his bout with Apollo Creed, eventually finding himself in a rematch with the champ. *Sylvester*

Stallone's character does one of the most unique marriage proposals as he asks Adrian, "I was wonderin' what you were doin' the next 40 or 50 years".

10. Kramer vs. Kramer

Ted Kramer's wife leaves him, allowing for a lost bond to be rediscovered between Ted and his son, Billy. But a heated custody battle ensues over the divorced couple's son, deepening the wounds left by the separation. *The film won five Academy Awards including Best Picture, Best Actor (Dustin Hoffman), Best Actress (Meryl Streep), and both Best Director and Best Writing/Screenplay (Robert Benton).*

Honorable Mention:

The Jerk

An idiotic man struggles to make it through life on his own in St. Louis. *Steve Martin is hilarious as rags - to riches - to rags, terminally uncool, Navin Johnson - a role he was well prepared for by his time on "Saturday Night Live".*

The question that boosted ratings.

"The thinking man's rock and roll..."
-David E. Ridge, 1979

For the ears

1979 Rock by the numbers, in no particular order...

On the Turntable
1. **The Wall** – Pink Floyd
2. **Rust Never Sleeps** – Neil Young
3. **Breakfast In America** – Supertramp
4. **Tusk** – Fleetwood Mac
5. **Damn The Torpedos** – Tom Petty and the Heartbreakers
6. **Cheap Trick At Budokan** – Cheap Trick
7. **Dire Straits** – Dire Straits

8. **Regatta de Blanc** – The Police
9. **Highway To Hell** – AC/DC
10. **London Calling** – The Clash
11. **The B-52's** – The B-52's
12. **The Long Run** – The Eagles
13. **In Through The Out Door** – Led Zeppelin
14. **Live Rust** – Neil Young
15. **Candy O** – The Cars

Guyana Punch Line

November 1978...Cult leader Jim Jones' followers commit mass suicide in Jonestown, Guyana. In total, 909 individuals died in Jonestown, all but two from apparent cyanide poisoning via a flavored drink, in an event termed "revolutionary suicide" by Jones and some Peoples Temple members on an audio tape of the event. This has led to the phrase *"drinking the Kool-Aid"*, referring to a person or group holding an unquestioned belief or philosophy without critical examination.

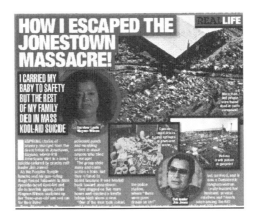

On the Radio
1. **Another Brick in the Wall, Part 2** - Pink Floyd
2. **London Calling** - The Clash
3. **Rapper's Delight** - The Sugarhill Gang
4. **Good Times** - Chic
5. **Dont Stop 'Til You Get Enough** - Michael Jackson
6. **We Are Family** - Sister Sledge
7. **Comfortably Numb** - Pink Floyd
8. **Hot Stuff** - Donna Summer
9. **Brass in Pocket** - The Pretenders
10. **Message in a Bottle** - The Police

On the tube 1979

1. Buck Rogers in the 25th Century (1979–1981)

A 20th century astronaut emerges out of 500 years of suspended animation into a future time to become Earth's greatest hero.

2. The Dukes of Hazzard (1979–1985)

The adventures of the fast-drivin', rubber-burnin' Duke boys of Hazzard County.

3. The Facts of Life (1979–1988)

A group of girls, attending a boarding school, tackle issues throughout teenage life and later adulthood.

4. Hart to Hart (1979–1984)

The globe-trotting adventures of amateur detectives Jonathan and Jennifer Hart.

5. Minder (1979–1994)

Arthur Daley, a small-time conman, hires former boxer Terry McCann to be his 'minder', so Terry can protect him (Arthur) from other, small-time, crooks.

6. Knots Landing (1979–1993)

The residents of Knots Landing, a coastal suburb of Los Angeles, deal with various issues such as infidelity, health scares, rape, murder, kidnapping, assassinations, drug smuggling, corporate intrigue and criminal investigations.

7. Prisoner: Cell Block H (1979–1986)

The lives of women behind bars in a female prison.

8. Archie Bunker's Place (1979–1983)

The further misadventures of Archie Bunker, now the owner of a local pub, and his regulars.

9. Benson (1979–1986)

Jessica Tate's sharp-tongued former butler, Benson DuBois, moves up in the world, becoming first the governor's "director of household affairs," then the state's budget director, then lieutenant governor and candidate for the executive mansion.

10. Tales of the Unexpected (1979–1988)

Dramatizations of many Roald Dahl short stories.

Honorable Mention:

SportsCenter (1979–)

Daily sports news, results, and features from the fledgling ESPN network on cable TV. The show is now a fan favorite.

Top TV Shows of 1979 (as measured by Nielsen Media Research)

1	60 Minutes	CBS
2	Three's Company	ABC
3	That's Incredible!	
4	Alice	
	M*A*S*H	
6	Dallas	
7	Flo	CBS
8	The Jeffersons	
9	The Dukes of Hazzard	
10	One Day at a Time	
11	Archie Bunker's Place	
12	Eight Is Enough	ABC
13	Taxi	
14	House Calls	CBS
	Real People	NBC
16	Little House on the Prairie	
17	Happy Days	ABC
18	CHiPs	NBC
19	Trapper John, M.D.	CBS
20	Charlie's Angels	ABC
	Barney Miller	
22	WKRP in Cincinnati	CBS
23	Benson	ABC
	The Love Boat	
25	Soap	

What in the world 1979

The Shah of Iran leaves his country after years of turmoil. Exiled Muslim leader Ayatollah Khomeini returns and declares an Islamic republic. Then in November, Iranian militants seize the U.S. embassy in Tehran and hold 52 Americans hostage for 444 days...releasing them on the day of President Reagan's Inauguration.

Electronic media.
Everything has changed. Nothing is different.

No Grain. No Games.

Carter Says U.S. Will Officially Boycott Olympics

In response to the Soviet invasion of Afghanistan in 1980, President Carter imposes an embargo on grain shipments to the USSR and boycotts the Moscow Olympics. Despite a lifetime's worth of training, U.S. Olympic Athletes would not get the chance to prove they are the best in the world...and by default, the Soviet Union (now Russia) would get - but not earn - the majority of medals.

From now on your Delta Chi Tau name is Pinto...

November 2, 1979 a plane crashes at Steak and Ale in Greenville, South Carolina, claiming five lives.

Mall Arcade

We cruised the mall. That was the deal. Parents could drop their kids off and enjoy a teen-free afternoon. At one end of this building was a special place...the arcade. Video games and pinball machines took tokens not quarters. An attendant dressed up in his arcaded regalia would make change and supply you with tokens. He also made sure you didn't glue a straightened paperclip to a token in order to trick the machine and play for free.

What in the world 1979

Margaret Thatcher, a conservative, becomes the first woman prime minister of Britain.

Chapter 10: Mean Green

"**Hey Kid, Catch!**" was a television commercial for Coca-Cola starring Pittsburgh Steelers defensive tackle "Mean" Joe Greene. The commercial debuted on October 1, 1979, and was re-aired multiple times, most notably during Super Bowl XIV in 1980. The 60-second commercial won a Clio Award for being one of the best television commercials of 1979.

During its planning and filming stages, McCann Erickson, the advertising agency that created the commercial, used the working title "Mean Joe Greene". The commercial was a part of Coca-Cola's "Have a Coke and a Smile" ad campaign of the late 1970's. The commercial's set-up and payoff is classic simple advertising.

After sustaining an injury during a football game, Greene is limping alone into the tunnel toward the Steelers' locker room when a young boy (played by Tommy Okon) comes up behind him offering his help, which Greene declines. After telling Greene that he still thinks he is the best, the boy offers him his bottle of Coke, which Greene refuses at first, but the boy wants him to have it; Greene sheepishly accepts it with thanks and drinks the entire bottle as the boy quietly says "See ya 'round" and slowly walks away. When Greene finishes the Coke he turns back to the boy and says "Hey, Kid...Catch," tossing his jersey (slung over his shoulder) to the surprised boy who happily says "Wow! Thanks, Mean Joe!". Greene casts a smile toward the boy before continuing his trek to the locker room.

Production Notes and Accolades

The campaign's art director was Roger Mosconi, the writer was Penny Hawkey, and the singers of the *"Coke and a Smile"* jingle were Jim Campbell, Don Thomas, Liz Corrigan, Shellie Littman, Arlene Martell, and Linda November. The footage was shot in May 1979 at a small stadium in Mount Vernon, New York, and the commercial first aired on October 1, 1979 on ABC's *"Monday Night Football"*, though its airing during Super Bowl XIV in 1980 brought it the most attention due to the program's enormous audience.

The commercial has been listed as one of the top ads of all time by multiple sources, including *TV Guide*. The ad later received worldwide acclaim when it was re-filmed in various countries using indigenous sports figures in each version.

Greene later recalled that in filming the commercial, it took several takes to get his final line in the commercial in without burping. "Between me belching and going to the men's room, it took three days to film it," Greene recalled.

In 2016 Joe reunited with Tommy Okon during a two-hour CBS special filmed at Apogee Stadium in Denton, Texas honoring Super Bowl's Greatest Commercials.

Parodies and homages

In 1983, the television show *"Newhart"* paid homage to the commercial in the first season episode *"A View from the Bench"* when a limping Celtics player throws his basketball shoes to Bob Newhart on his way to the locker room.

A *"Sesame Street"* segment featuring Gordon (as the football player), giving a big towel to a kid, which then has the number seven on it as a way to show the number seven as the number of the day.

In 2003, in the television show *"Frasier"* the character Niles gives a child a handkerchief in a similar manner after a good performance at an elementary-school assembly about the importance of cleanliness.

During Super Bowl XLIII in 2009, Coca-Cola aired a parody to the ad to promote its Coca-Cola Zero brand, starring former Steelers player Troy Polamalu in Greene's role. Continuing an ongoing theme in promotion for the beverage, the ad is interrupted by Coca-Cola "brand managers" who accuse Polamalu of "stealing" their commercial, prompting the safety to tackle one of them and give the child their shirt.

In 2011, an episode of *"SportsNation"* on ESPN2 briefly parodied this commercial which featured sportscaster Michelle Beadle in Greene's role. In the commercial, after finishing the soda, instead of the jersey, she "accidentally" throws the empty soda bottle back to the child as it breaks on the wall at the end and then apologizes after that "mishap". In addition, the commercial tried to look like the late 1970's/early 1980's font titles with the words

"Facebook.com/SportsNation" and "Have Some *"SportsNation"* and a smile" and "Sports is Life".

An advertisement for the Fox television drama series *House*, first aired during Super Bowl XLV, parodies the original commercial with a similar scene in which Dr. Gregory House, played by Hugh Laurie, throws his cane to a young fan played by Preston Bailey.

In 2012, Greene reprised his role in a Downy Unstopables ad for Super Bowl XLVI entitled *"Stinky"*, where Amy Sedaris rejects Greene's jersey because it smelled.

Blockbuster Video. Please be kind...rewind.

Corporal punishment.

The offense: Orchestrating a golf club throwing contest in Ms. Clayton's P.E. class.

The sentence: 3 days trash detail.

Commuted to: 3 licks from the Principal.

Other books by Adam Fisher:

"The True Diary of An Adman"
A first-hand account of the crazy world of advertising as told by a real Adman. This collection of stories will make you laugh…and think.

"Speaking of Recovery"
Stories of the path to sobriety. Filled with humor, insight, and hope.

Available on Amazon.

Special Thanks to Howard Hunt for cover artwork.

About the artist:

Howard studied many forms of art at the University of South Carolina, but photography and painting have always kept his interest. Artistic creativity and an eye for details has set him apart from the competition.

Whether he's headed to France, Costa Rica, New Orleans, or just taking a kayak trip down the Saluda River, Howard's excitement for finding a stimulating image to capture on canvas or on film remains the same.

Recently his art has been accepted in locally and nationally recognized juror art shows. His work can spark a new idea for you.

View a complete portfolio at hhuntart.com.

Howard Hunt Art and Photography. When image matters.

Made in the USA
Monee, IL
03 March 2020